NINO PIRROTTA

DON GIOVANNI'S PROGRESS:
A RAKE GOES TO THE OPERA

Translated by Harris S. Saunders, Jr.

Marsilio
New York

CONTENTS

ISBN hc 0-941419-71-1
ISBN pb 0-941419-94-0

PRINTED IN ITALY

DON GIOVANNI'S PROGRESS
A Rake Goes to the Opera

Preface and Dedication

This essay, which the cordial friends who direct the *Musica critica* series have induced me to publish, makes no pretense to being a critical or scientific contribution, but is instead a work of dissemination. It originated as a series of lecture notes for a university course I taught in 1973–74, a course designed for students who did not intend to specialize in the study of music history but rather to draw cultural enrichment from it, a course during which the choice of one of the most famous dramatic themes ever served to have students listen to music of various styles, periods, and genres. The course in fact extended far beyond the eighteenth century to encompass the opera *Kamenniy gost'* by Alexander Dargomïzhsky and Alexander Pushkin (1866–69), the symphonic poem *Don Juan* by Richard Strauss (1888–89), and, on the same subject if not a direct derivation, *The Rake's Progress* by Igor Stravinsky (1947–51). But the text presented as an aid to students concentrated on the seventeenth and eighteenth centuries, chiefly as a contribution to the recognition of the historical context of Mozart's opera. In its present form, it also encompasses later essays: a paper I presented at a conference under the title "The Traditions of Don Juan Plays and Comic Operas" (held in 1981 at the Royal Musical Association in London and later published in volume 107 of the *Proceedings of the Royal Musical Association*) and the article "Il sorriso di Mozart" (originally intended for a miscellany in honor of Giovanni Macchia in 1983 and later included in the volume *Scelte poetiche di musicisti*).

The figure and adventures of Don Giovanni occupy an important place in the history of theater and of European culture. Anyone interested in deepening his knowledge of the theatrical works in various genres that arose from this theme and the reverberations this theme engendered in the Romantic imagination will find a valuable orientation in the succinct but illuminating essay by Giovanni Macchia, *Vita av venture e morte di Don Giovanni* (Bari: Laterza, 1966; new edition, Turin: Einaudi, 1978) and in his valuable complementary appendix of seventeenth-century texts on this theme. Even more vast is the literature on Mozart and his *Don Giovanni*: in this regard, I will limit myself to citing one recent investigation, *Lettura del Don Giovanni* (Turin: Einaudi, 1988), one of Massimo Mila's last works, and among his most felicitous. I should also cite the important study by Stefan Kunze, *Don Giovanni vor Mozart* (Munich: Fink, 1972), which contains synopses and excerpts from various libretti and scores and the complete text of *Don Giovanni o sia Il convitato di pietra* by Giuseppe Gazzaniga, produced in Venice in 1787 with music by Giuseppe Gazzaniga a few months before the premiere of Mozart's opera in Prague. Stefan Kunze's ample study of *Il teatro di Mozart* (originally *Mozarts Opern*) has now appeared in this same series.

The task of retrieving and transcribing the music of various operas before Mozart's was facilitated through access to the collection of microfilms of manuscripts and rare prints of early Italian music begun some years ago under the direction of Luigi Ronga in what was then called the Istituto di Storia della musica dell'Università La Sapienza di Roma, which is today supported with funds provided by the Consiglio nazionale delle ricerche. Thus we were able to transcribe passages from the scores of *L'empio punito* by

Alessandro Melani (1669) and *Il convitato di pietra* by Giacomo Tritto (1784) for performance in class; my friends Raoul Meloncelli and Ariella Lanfranchi helped me greatly in these presentations as they have through all my years of teaching. For the study of *Il convitato di pietra* by Bertati and Gazzaniga (1787) I was able to use the edition that Maestro Guido Turchi drew up for a performance by RAI, the Italian national television (this edition is not in the public domain); but the score of this opera is now accessible in an edition by Stefan Kunze: Giuseppe Gazzaniga, *Don Giovanni* (Kassel: Bärenreiter, 1974). Of the other eighteenth-century operas discussed in my text, either the scores have not survived (this is so for *La pravità castigata* by Bambini and *Il convitato di pietra* by Righini; for the latter I have no confirmation of a score existing in Budapest), or I have deliberately excluded them because they are unrepresentative of their composers, and because it is highly improbable that Mozart and Da Ponte had any inkling of them. For the musical examples, including Melani's seventeenth-century work, I have limited the realization of the basso continuo to the minimum necessary for the harmonies or to reinforce those harmonies already present in the obbligato instruments; for Tritto's opera I have instead offered a reduction of the orchestral accompaniment.

Finally, to complement the bibliographic notes above and those that will be found in the text, I should cite the editions of Mozart's score to which the reader can refer: *Il dissoluto punito ossia Il Don Giovanni*, edited by Alfred Einstein (Leipzig: Eulenburg, 1930), and the edition by Wolfgang Plath and Wolfgang Rehm, *Il dissoluto punito . . .* , in the *Neue Ausgabe sämtlicher Werke,* vol. 18.

Once before I dedicated a volume of mine to three dearest, most unforgettable friends; today, as I grow older, and as painful separations repeat themselves, I feel the need to remember three other recently departed friends who contributed greatly to my studies. I therefore dedicate this work to Nanie Bridgman, whose smiling affability I first learned to appreciate long ago in 1938; to Lele D'Amico, as generous in the warmth of his friendship as in the vivid illumination of his intelligence; and to Massimo Mila, serene and sincere apostle of a civilized polity and musical culture. With affection and thanks.

Rome, February 1991
N. P.

CHAPTER ONE: THE SEVENTEENTH CENTURY

1. The Myth of Don Giovanni in European Theater

With the passage of time, the name of Don Giovanni has come to symbolize an excessive propensity toward eroticism, usually condemned by morality, religion, or prudery, but also occasionally exalted as the expression of a vital daemon, or ennobled as the unfulfilled aspiration toward an unattainable absolute beauty. It has not always been so. In its earliest form and throughout the seventeenth century and most of the eighteenth, eroticism was only one of many aspects in a portrait whose fundamental note, often underscored in titles, is impiety and disbelief, which is inevitably destined for the terrible final punishment of eternal damnation.

In the uncertain prehistory of this character, who has been so much the subject of myth, the only documented precedent, credible because of its proximity in time and place and its significant parallels, is the story of a certain Count Leonzio, described in the context of the Counter-Reformation as a corrupt disbeliever, who had as preceptor none other than Niccolò Machiavelli. In the Jesuit writing chosen by Giovanni Macchia to document this tradition, a passage taken from the theologian Paul Zehentner's *Promontorium Malae Spei Impiis Periculose Navigantibus Propositum* [Argument For the Impious Ones Navigating Dangerously the Cape of Bad Hope] there is an account of a theatrical performance in which Leonzio, like Hamlet, apostrophizes a skull and defies him, inviting him mockingly to a banquet to entertain his dinner guests with a debate over whether the mortal bodies of men enclose an immortal soul; unexpectedly, the skeleton appears at the banquet and drags away the scoffer to eternal punishment, amid scenes of terror in which Machiavelli cuts a poor figure in the company of those who will follow him in this role, such as Catalinón, Sganarelle, and Leporello.[1] Zehentner's account is dated 1643 but refers to a performance that he attended in Ingolstadt in 1615, on the basis of which he claims it was an older story written in Italian. No more than fifteen years later, Don Giovanni officially enters literary history with a comedy similar in its moralistic intent and exemplary conclusion, *El burlador de Sevilla y convidado de piedra* [The Trickster of Seville and the Stone Guest].

El burlador de Sevilla, printed anonymously in 1630 in Barcelona, had already been performed years before by a company headed by Roque de Figueroa. For a long time it was attributed to Calderón de la Barca or Lope de Vega, but today it is ascribed to Gabriel Téllez (1584?–1648), better known under the pseudonym Tirso de Molina. It unfolds in three *jornadas*, which correspond only loosely to our concept of "act." Labels are limited to indicating the entrance and exit of characters and hardly ever include references to time or place; within each *jornada* it is clear that the action passes repeatedly from one place to another (one envisions a casual staging); from the changes in place and the nature of events it emerges that in a number of instances several days have passed between one episode and the next. The action piles episode upon episode with exuberant but disorderly richness, without excessive concern for coherence or verisimilitude; but its urgent rhythm, its succession of stratagems on the part of the characters and the author, the variety of dissimulations perpetrated to the harm of men and women dramatize the contrast between a life lived moment to moment without thought for the future, in the fierce pleasure of the jest and of deception, and the horrible end of damnation. This highlights the intention of giving an exemplary value to the parable of the cynical libertine led (or better, predestined, given that predestination was one of Tirso's favorite themes) to eternal punishment, an intention further confirmed by the preference here, as in successive elaborations of the theme, for titles that refer to the final punishment: *Il convitato di pietra* [The Stone Guest], or *L'ateista fulminato* [The Atheist Struck Down By Lightning], or *L'empio punito* [The Rake Punished].

El burlador is not without its duplications: two kings appear with their ambassadors and counselors; Don Giovanni betrays two friends by insinuating himself with their lovers; there are two women of the lower classes (one surrounded by fishermen, the other by peasants) whom Don Giovanni seduces and then precipitously abandons; there are two banquets at which the statues of the man he killed intervenes; all these are carefully developed through to the very end. Remarkable also is the number of Don Giovanni's erotic enterprises, perhaps only one of which (the conquest of Donna Anna) falls short of success. But his amatory interest is only one of a number of character traits; most distinctive is his thoughtless egoism and his sadistic relish in deceiving ("burlar") men and women, including his own relatives, for his own enjoyment and advantage. Those around him are not much better: Don Pedro Tenorio deceives his king and Don Ottavio to save his nephew; at least two other male characters (Don Diego Tenorio and the Marquis de la Mota) have committed their own love transgressions; and none of the four women, not even Donna Anna, is a model of virtue. If Tirso is the author of this comedy, he expresses a profound misogyny; and no less profound, even if perhaps unintentional, is the squalor that emanates from his presentation of the life of the aristocracy at this time (the placement in a vague historic past deceives no one): the despotism that grants and withholds favors with equal facility, the privileges of caste, the concept of honor created for the sole sake of formality and appearance. (The two episodes among the common folk are brief diversions without any serious claim toward realism.)

It is useful to summarize this overabundant material, which later works did not hesitate to use freely.

Act I: (Court of Naples) During a nocturnal tryst, Duchess Isabella has given herself to a man whom she believed to be Duke Ottavio. The man now stops her from lighting a candle, and at the altercation that follows the king appears; the unknown man completely wrapped in his cloak and remanded into the custody of Don Pedro Tenorio reveals himself to be Don Pedro's nephew Don Giovanni; Don Pedro convinces his nephew to flee, after which Don Pedro casts suspicion upon Duke Ottavio, Isabella's beloved. (*Duke Ottavio's Palace*) Don Pedro comes to arrest Ottavio, who is more grieved than anything by Isabella's betrayal. Don Pedro lets him flee also. (*Spanish Coast*) Don Giovanni and his servant Catalinón arrive, having saved themselves in their flight from Naples by swimming to shore after their ship has been wrecked; while Catalinón goes in search of help, Don Giovanni revives in the arms of the fishermaid Tisbea (who is already aware of his noble rank) and courts her. (*Court of Castile*) Don Gonzalo de Ulloa informs the king of his mission as ambassador to Lisbon; the king wants to reward him by giving his daughter in marriage to Don Giovanni.

(*Shore*) Don Giovanni orders Catalinón to have horses ready for flight as soon as he has conquered Tisbea; the girl is easily induced to welcome him into her cottage. Fishermen are celebrating on the shore, but their musical merrymaking is interrupted by Tisbea's laments after she realizes Don Giovanni has fled.

Act II: (Court of Castile) Don Diego Tenorio, Don Giovanni's father, confesses to the king that his son caused a scandal in Naples. The king limits himself to punishing Don Giovanni by exiling him to a village near Seville; he has doubts about the wisdom of the promised marriage with Donna Anna de Ulloa, and in fact a moment later promises her to Duke Ottavio, another fugitive from Naples. *(A Street in Seville)* Don Giovanni and Catalinón first meet Duke Ottavio (who is yet unaware that Don Giovanni was the man discovered with Isabella) and then the Marquis de la Mota; the marquis reports to Don Giovanni piquant facts about ladies and courtesans whom the two of them have frequented, but then confesses having fallen in love with Donna Anna de Ulloa, before whose house they are standing. Their conversation is noted from inside the house, and someone hands Don Giovanni a note intended for the marquis: Donna Anna has learned that she is promised to an unknown man and wants to meet the marquis at eleven o'clock that evening. Don Giovanni reads the message out loud, giving twelve o'clock as the time of the meeting. Other encounters follow: Don Diego Tenorio admonishes his son to change his way of life; at night the marquis returns with musicians to perform a serenade. Don Giovanni borrows the marquis' cloak purportedly to help him gain access to the house of one of the courtesans they had discussed earlier; instead it helps him enter Donna Anna's house at eleven o'clock; he is discovered and kills Don Gonzalo, who had run to his daughter's defense. The corpse has hardly been carried into the house when the unknowing marquis returns, takes back his cloak, goes toward his tryst, and is arrested for murder. *(Court of Castile)* The king orders that the marquis be tried and decapitated and that a mausoleum be built to the Commendatore Ulloa. *(Countryside)* Catalinón attends a rustic banquet with music and song; Don Giovanni arrives and immediately takes his place beside Aminta, the bride, despite the protests of Batricio, the groom.

Act III: (Countryside) Don Giovanni convinces Batricio to renounce Aminta, claiming that she has been in love with him for a long time; Aminta complains to a girlfriend that the nobleman has made Batricio jealous. Don Giovanni tells Aminta's father that he wants to marry her tomorrow, but in the meantime orders Catalinón to have horses ready by nightfall. At night, he speaks to Aminta, convinces her with promises of marriage, and is welcomed into her house. *(Tarragona)* Isabella travels toward Seville; she does not regret that the scandal is forcing her to marry Don Giovanni, only that she has besmirched her own name; she encounters Tisbea who laments Don Giovanni's deception. *(The Commendatore's Tomb)* Don Giovanni is warned by Catalinón that Duke Ottavio and the Marquis de la Mota are looking for him to avenge the wrongs they have suffered at his hands. They recognize the tomb. Mocking the epigraph, which demands vengeance, Don Giovanni invites the statue to dinner and to a duel afterward. *(Don Giovanni's Dwelling)* Dinner is being prepared. There is knocking at the door, and the servants who go to answer return one after the other in fear; Don Giovanni goes to welcome the statue. All tremble, but Don Giovanni wants dinner to proceed as usual including the accompaniment of song; dinner over, it is now the statue's turn to invite Don Giovanni before slowly departing. *(Court of Castile)* The king orders Don Giovanni to wed Isabella and Donna Anna to wed Duke Ottavio; this placates Ottavio who had come to demand justice. Left alone, Ottavio listens to the laments of Aminta and her father. *(Street)* It is night and Don Giovanni tells Catalinón he was well received by the king and will wed Isabella tomorrow. They enter the church, which houses the Commendatore's tomb, and encounter his statue, while pages dressed in black sing lugubrious songs as they prepare a black table with reptiles for food and vinegar for drink. Catalinón trembles, but Don Giovanni accepts the invitation to shake the statue's hand, which makes him feel as if he is all afire; there is no more time for repentance; an earthquake destroys the tomb and Don Giovanni along with it. *(Court of Castile)* Catalinón recounts what he saw. One by one the victims of Don Giovanni's ridicule arrive, and the marriages that had come to naught in his wake are rearranged; in memory of the event, the king orders that the Commendatore's tomb be rebuilt in Madrid.

The increasing vogue for Spanish theater in Italy resulted in Tirso's *Burlador* being taken up by Italian actors and authors. Benedetto Croce cites a performance in Naples in 1636 by the same Roque de Figueroa company mentioned above;[2] but according to a more recent source the same text had already been performed in 1625 by a company headed by Pedro Osorio and Gregorio Laredo.[3] The now lost translation made by Osorio Giliberto at some uncertain date was also Neapolitan; he entitled the work *Il convitato di pietra*.[4] Neither is it easy to assign a date to *Il convitato di pietra, opera regia et esemplare,* printed anonymously in several cities; perhaps it stems from Giacinto Andrea Cicognini (1606–ca. 1650; prolific writer of stage works including three opera libretti). More than a translation, it is a reworking already adapted to the practices of Italian theater: the peasant girl Aminta has become Brunetta, daughter of the Doctor (a Bolognese mask) and promised bride of Pantalone.[5] The same title was used for a later reworking (Naples, 1678) by Andrea Perrucci (1651–1704), another author of dramatic works in various genres,[6] including opera libretti, and also the author of a treatise entitled *Dell'arte rappresentativa, premeditata e all'improvviso* [On the Art of Acting Both Written and Improvised Plays] (Naples, 1699). But more important than literary or semiliterary translations or reworkings, Tirso's parable experienced good fortune and bad in the use and abuse made of it by the commedia dell'arte.

Commedia dell'arte is not a genre, but a way of doing theater: it is the art of theatrical improvisation, which is also referred to in the title of Andrea Perrucci's treatise. It is the way of acting that had prevailed in Italy since the second half of the sixteenth century, when the non-professionals, to whom Renaissance theater had largely been entrusted, came increasingly to be replaced by actors (i.e., "comici") who were professionals ("dell'arte"), and who, instead of giving occasional performances, aimed at profiting from the opportunity to attract a large public to a continuous series of performances. To respond to the public's demand for an ever richer and more varied repertoire they rejected the practice of committing to memory a large number of literarily elaborate texts that would be repeated each time invariably (the "premeditated art" of Perrucci); they instead adopted the system of agreeing beforehand on the outlines of what was to happen in each scene of the stage work (whether tragedy or comedy) and to create the dialogue extemporaneously, in part using passages or tirades memorized and readapted in analogous situations in different works, in part with true improvisations. Thus they formed, above all but not exclusively in comedies, a special style of recitation based on caricature, on frequent repetition wordplay and sight gags of proven comic success (the so-called *lazzi*), and very often on the coarse comedy of the bastinade or on acrobatics.

A parallel aspect, born from the repetition and proven success of particular approaches and comic characterizations suited to particular actors, was the creation of an entire series of characters infused with characteristics that were especially congenial to particular actors. These characters reappeared from one stage work to another (it did not matter whether it was tragedy, comedy or pastoral) involved in the most varied conditions or situations, but giving the audience the relish of recognizing unaltered under the same name their characteristic clothing and dialect, their physical signs and their caricatures or character flaws, already announced before those of the rest of the cast in each new stage work. Thus the typical masks gradually arose: most—like Zanni, Arlecchino, or Pulcinella (the list of names and the variety of types is much broader)—involved servants, or characters belonging in some way or other to the lower social classes; others, like Pantalone and the Doctor, in roles as pretentious, pompous, and ridiculous old bourgeois.

Various surviving commedia dell'arte scenarios treat the story of Don Giovanni (at times changing the names and emphasizing aspects of the story differently). The above-mentioned volume by Giovanni Macchia reprints several of these texts in an appendix;[7] but the number of surviving scenarios is not in proportion to the infinitely greater number of performances of a subject that offered such ample latitude to the actors' inspiration. In general, these scenarios tended to simplify the plot, suppressing some of the characters or conflating into one the characteristics of several. In part, this was done to assign the roles equally among the reduced number of actors in particular companies, but also because a minimal plot sufficed for the actors to inflate the stage work with all types of buffoonery. At other times, as in the scenarios published by Macchia entitled *L'ateista fulminato*,[8] the availability or lack of availability of particular stage effects probably induced the elimination of the appearance of the Commendatore's statue (and his earlier death in a duel), replacing it with a device whereby a temple opens to reveal the statue of one of the characters offended by Don Giovanni (here called Count Aurelio) who in well-rhymed admonishments invites him to repent; this device is repeated several times until the heavens finally open with thunder and lightning, it grows dark, and a bolt of lightning strikes before Aurelio's feet, who immediately sinks while the temple closes (hence the title variant). Particularly instructive are notes taken by an Arlecchino who enjoyed great success in Paris, Giuseppe Domenico Biancolelli (1636–1688);[9] among other things, these notes already include (as in the *Convitato di pietra* attributed to Cicognini) the jest of the long roll containing the list of Don Giovanni's feminine conquests; Arlecchino is supposed to show this to the most recent victim, but he throws it into the auditorium instead, inviting the spectators with a scornful expression to check if it contains the names of some of their relatives. Arlecchino, naturally, is Don Giovanni's servant here, a role already important in Tirso's Catalinón that had grown larger because of the general tendency of the commedia dell'arte to highlight the comic parts more than the serious (Don Giovanni figured among the serious parts, if for no other reason than his social rank). To the same tendency is attributable the fact that the titles alluding to castigation (often confirmed in a final vision of hell) provided a protective moral defense, which opened the way for all types of sly winks and salacious double entendres accentuating the libertine and erotic aspects of the protagonist and his adventures.

Commedia dell'arte acting troupes carried their theater to every part of Europe and enjoyed particular success in France beginning in the second half of the sixteenth century; toward the end of the next century, they even succeeded in institutionalizing themselves in the Théâtre des Italiens. In writing his *Don Juan ou Le Festin de pierre* [Don Juan or The Stone Guest] (1665), Molière may have had some direct knowledge of the Spanish prototype by Tirso de Molina; he certainly came into contact, either in Paris or in the provinces, with the versions presented by Italian commedia dell'arte troupes, from whom he may have borrowed elements that give the servant Sganarelle—his favorite creation—his particular comic profile.[10] Without excluding the possibility of earlier performances, we are certain that a *Convitato di pietra*, referred to by French chroniclers as *Le Festin de pierre*, was presented in Paris in 1657 (the company, led by Domenico Locatelli, performed in Italian).[11] But aside from this production, from which may derive the above-mentioned scenario by Giuseppe Domenico Biancolelli,[12] two comedies by two other French author-actors preceded Molière's comedy. Both are in verse and both are entitled *Le Festin de pierre ou Le Fils criminel* [The Stone Guest or The Criminal Son]: the one by Dorimond, a pseudonym for Nicolas Druoin (ca. 1628–ca. 1673), was presented in Lyon in 1658 and printed there in 1659, and the other by Claude Deschamps, known as Villiers (1601–1681), was presented in Paris in 1659, the actor assuming his favorite role of Philippin, Don Giovanni's servant here. After Molière, another author-actor who belonged to a rival company, Claude La Rose, known as Rosimond, presented in Paris in 1669 a *Nouveau Festin de pierre ou L'Athéiste foudroyé* [The New Stone Guest or The Atheist Struck by Lightning] (published in 1670). As may be deduced from the alternative titles, Don Juan's principal sin in the first two comedies are the wrongs committed against his father and family, while Rosimond's comedy highlights above all his impiety and atheism.[13]

Molière's comedy demands special consideration because of the stature of the author and the elements that it transmitted to eighteenth-century imitators. It should be kept in mind, however, that the original version does not survive among the various editions that have come down to us: the comedy performed for the first time in February 1665 immediately drew violent criticism and had to be withdrawn; it was later published in an addition to the *Oeuvres posthumes* of the complete edition of Molière's works of 1682, in a version first censored by the editors and then more broadly by the official censors.[14] The work appeared onstage not in prose, as the author had conceived it, but in a censored edition in limpid alexandrines by Thomas Corneille, the only edition performed in the eighteenth and a good part of the nineteenth century. Perhaps closer to the original text is the edition that appeared in 1683 in Amsterdam under the title *Le Festin de pierre . . . Edition nouvelle et toute différente de celle qui a paru jusqu'à present* [The Stone Guest: A New and Entirely Different Edition from the One That Has Already Appeared]; the latter restores among other things the abuse of power that Don Juan exercises over a poor man when he tries to make him blaspheme in order to obtain alms.[15]

Molière's vocation for the comedy of character and of manner rather than the comedy of intrigue is clear. The unusual formulation of the title directs attention toward the role of the *grand seigneur méchant homme* [great lord yet wicked man] who believes in nothing and to whom everything seems permissible (a terrible thing, Sganarelle says of him already in the first scene). The nonchalance of apparent generosity that makes him intervene to help a stranger assaulted by robbers is nothing other than overweening pride masked by a sense of honor. Once more eroticism plays an important part in the five acts, but not the main one: the character himself confesses that his principal motive is a taste for novelty and conquest. Sganarelle for his part sees as his master's main fault the promises he makes without any intention of fulfilling them, his use of the sacrament of marriage as an expedient of conquest without any intention of respecting it (from Sganarelle stems the definition of Don Juan as "épouseur à toutes mains" [suitor after every hand] and "épouseur du genre humain" [suitor of the human race]). The height is reached in Don Juan's sudden conversion to a most hypocritical and bigoted piety, which permits him to take refuge behind false scruples (here Molière has personal targets and returns to the motive of *Tartuffe*, whose performances had been banned the year before). Two episodes that elsewhere almost always figure prominently, the murder of the Commendatore and the shipwreck, are hardly mentioned in the dialogue: the murder, whose motives and circumstances are not explained, took place six months before the comedy begins, and Don Juan has recently been pardoned for having committed it; the shipwreck, documented in passing in the conversation of various characters, frustrates Don Juan's plan to seize the opportunity a boat ride presents to ravish a girl who is too much in love with her fiancé (neither of whom ever appear onstage): "La tendresse visible de leurs mutuelles ardeurs me donna de l'émotion; . . . et je me figurai un plaisir extrême à pouvoir troubler leur intelligence et rompre cet attachement, dont la délicatesse de mon coeur se tenait offensée" ["The clear tenderness of their mutual ardor moved me; . . . and I imagined I would greatly enjoy troubling their minds and breaking this attachment, whose delicacy so offended my heart"].

Also antecedent to the action is the conquest of Elvire, his only successful conquest in—or rather, before—the comedy; with the peasant girls Mathurine and Charlotte, whom he courts one after the other, Don Juan does not achieve complete success because of the headlong rush of events. Elvire is a new character (even though she combines characteristics of Isabella and Tisbea from Tirso's comedy); Don Juan has plucked her from a convent through marriage and then immediately abandoned her. From the beginning of the comedy, she is searching for him and for an explanation for his abandonment; she introduces a pathetic note destined to remain part of the tradition. Her two brothers, however, do not remain part of the tradition; they also pursue Don Juan to force him to make up for the offense. Just as tenaciously remembered and imitated, even if of secondary importance in the economy of the comedy, are the blows Don Juan deals Pierrot, the rustic in love with Charlotte, and the expedient by which Don Juan holds at bay Charlotte and Mathurine, who meet each other before his seduction has achieved its goal: to each one he lets it be known that the other is crazy.

Like most of the Italian and French actors who preceded him, Molière reserved for himself the part of Sganarelle, Don Juan's valet (Don Juan has two other colorless servants). Sganarelle is attached to Don Juan through greed and fear, but from the very first scene he describes his master as "le plus grand scélerat que la terre ait jamais porté, un enragé, un chien, un diable, un Turc, un hérétique . . ." ["the greatest scoundrel the earth has ever seen, a madman, a dog, a devil, a Turk, a heretic . . ."] and even without the jest of the list he anticipates Leporello in the description of his master's undiscriminating tastes: "dame, demoiselle, bourgeoise, paysanne, il ne trouve rien de trop chaud ni de trop froid pour lui; et si je disais le nom de toutes celles qu'il a épousées en divers lieux, ce serait un chapitre à durer jusques au soir . . ." ["lady, young girl, from the city, or the countryside, he finds nothing too hot or too cold for him; and if I were to name all the ones he has married in various places, I would be reciting this chapter until evening comes on . . ."]. Critics have noted that his part may be more extensive than Don Juan's, and at least two of his character traits contributed to the comedy being censored: his superstitious belief in the "moine bourru" (a type of werewolf) and the cynicism with which in the presence of the spectacle of divine punishment he finds nothing other to lament than his lost wages: "Mes gages! mes gages!"[16]

2. *Don Giovanni Goes to the Opera*

L'empio punito, libretto by Pippo Acciaiuoli (apparently set to verse by Giovanni Apolloni) and set to music by Alessandro Melani, is the earliest documented musical incarnation of the myth of Don Giovanni. A letter by Salvator Rosa to his friend Giovanni Battista Ricciardi dated 25 January 1669 already makes mention of it,[17] while also documenting how Roman operatic practice, after the passing of Barberini patronage,[18] had come to approach the pseudo-commercial organization that preceded the opening of the first public opera house in Rome, the Tordinona, in 1671. The letter refers to the stage work not with the title as it appears on the printed libretto but with the one used more recently in spoken theater ("*Il convitato di pietra*, in spite of all the novelty"); and informs us that a "society of cavaliers" prepared it at the great expense of "from five to six thousand *scudi*." The venue, at one time a princely palace (that of the Conestabile Colonna in Borgo) seems to have been a semipublic theater, i.e., open to the highest aristocracy; the first performance took place on 17 February under the aegis of Queen Christina of Sweden, who reserved the theater for herself and a densely packed audience of cardinals whom she invited. From another source we learn that "Her Majesty praised the music, the stage sets and the ballets highly, but it seems that she was bored by the length of the opera, since when Cardinal Rospigliosi inquired how Her Majesty liked the opera, she responded: 'It's *Il convitato di pietra*.'"[20] Thus she also had easily penetrated the operatic disguise, even though presented "in suave verses (in which 'Amore' is capitalized, and shepherds and princesses, servants and masters speak the same language), within the feigned portrait of an idyllic and literary nature."[21]

Born in Rome and educated at the Collegio Romano, Pippo [Filippo] Acciaiuoli belonged, however, to a well-off family of the Florentine nobility and was also the brother of a cardinal; earlier he had distinguished himself in Florence where, as a member of the Accademia degli Immobili, he had among other things danced with many other members of the nobility who took part in the elaborate intermezzi in Cavalli's *Ipermestra* of 1658. He had an adventurous spirit that drove him to many years of travel in far-away, even exotic, lands and he enjoyed the esteem of high social and cultural circles (he was patronized by Ferdinando de' Medici and later Christina of Sweden, and was finally also welcomed among the Arcadians). Returning to Rome in 1667, he quickly revealed his passion for musical theater. He wrote and successfully staged (30 January 1668) the opera *Il Girello*, *dramma musicale burlesco*, set to music by another of the Melani brothers, Jacopo (they all belonged to a family of musicians of high standing in Pistoia).[22] Two tendencies have been noted in his theatrical activity, though they have not always been clearly distinguished from each other: the tendency to anticipate comic opera, apparent in *Girello* and probably prompted by his exposure in Florence to Giovanni Andrea Moniglia and the latter's *drammi civili* (some of which were set to music by Jacopo Melani); and the other more pronounced tendency in *L'empio punito*, to design grandiose stage effects and to use spectacular machines that he himself probably invented (which he would later use in a lyric theater for marionettes).[23] The choice of theme of *L'empio punito*, which had well-known comic antecedents, also evinces the first tendency, which is confirmed by the ample comic part given to Bibi, the servant of the character who now assumes the role of Don Giovanni, Acrimante.[24]

In accord with the second tendency, the plot of *L'empio punito* does not take place in Naples, Seville, and Castile as usual, and in an unspecified but recent time; it is transported instead to a fantastic operatic, pseudo-classical clime, to Pella at the court of the king of Macedonia, under the invented name of Atrace. In the libretto are listed twelve changes of scene (that must have taken place before the eyes of the spectators)[25] and three machines ("A vessel that sinks," "Charon's barque," and "The flight of the statue of Tidemo"), but to this must be added several other statues that move and later also dance in an *intermedio*.[26] And to the *intermedii* with the statues must be added, also in *intermedii* between the acts, dances of Moors and monsters.

The beginning is new with respect to the tradition: in the stables of "the king's cousin" Cloridoro, a chorus of stableboys provides the background first for the song of Ipomene, "the king's sister," who has come to search out her lover before he leaves for the hunt, and later for the two lovers' duet. But soon the first change of scene carries us to "Woods with open sea" and to the first of the stage marvels, the shipwreck of the vessel. To the woods on this shore has arrived, we known not how, Atamira, daughter of the king of Corinth, and, like Elvira, she is in search of her beloved unfaithful spouse. She lends aid to the two victims of the shipwreck, one of whom she recognizes as her own Acrimante, "cousin of the king of Corinth," who seduced her and deceived her with a false matrimony. Acrimante harshly rejects her; Bibi, his servant, first has a few jests and then quickly announces the arrival of two shepherdesses:

Allegrezza, padrone,	Rejoice, master!
tien pur lesta la penna:	Hold your pen ready.
se non erra la vista,	If my eyes do not deceive me,
ecco roba da scriver nella lista!	Here's something to add to the list!

Acrimante asks one of these shepherdesses for shelter and accompanies her, after having once more rejected Atamira. Bibi also leaves after having comically admonished Atamira about the fake beards of the witnesses at her wedding. Sad and exhausted, Atamira falls asleep, not without having first sung a lament. Thus the arrival of King Atrace, with Cloridoro and retinue, can provide the occasion for another conventional operatic scene, a dialogue with a sleeping person (we will have another one later on with the sleeping Acrimante who has a dialogue with Atamira and with a terrified Bibi who believes him dead). Having finally awoken, Atamira does not reveal herself to the king (she says to herself, "I am a betrayed lover and a queen"); but Atrace wants her at his court:

e a ciò che in avvenire	So that in future
nella mia Reggia un doppio Sol risplenda,	In my palace a double sun will shine;
dell'Infanta Ipomene	Await the Infanta Ipomene
entro le stanze il mio ritorno attenda	In my chambers.

Thus are set up the fundamental elements of the action: two couples—one in accord (Ipomene and Cloridoro), the other in discord (Atamira and Atrace)—along with Acrimante who, when received at Atrace's court, falls in love with Ipomene and using deceit does all he can to win her. The instruments of deception are Bibi and Ipomene's old wet-nurse, Delfa, whom Bibi pretends to be in love with; but this plot is finally foiled by the intervention of Tidemo, "Ipomene's tutor and counselor," who, however, is killed in a duel and becomes the instrument of divine punishment in the usual scene of mockery toward the statue and of the opening of the earth to swallow the mocker (the flight of the statue is an unnecessary addition of Acciaiuoli's scenographic imagination). Atrace, the king, is basically, a secondary character, but, having fallen in love with Atamira at first sight (right after having sung of the joy of being free of every amorous heartache) he will end up marrying her in the finale, associating his own wedding with that of Ipomene and Cloridoro.

This is the essential nucleus of the plot, but numerous side episodes slow it down and draw it out: the frequent comic duets between Bibi and Delfa; the soliloquies of King Atrace, who beyond lamenting his own unrequited love for Atamira, suspects that he himself killed Tidemo with an improvident and anachronistic pistol shot; the jealous remonstrances of Cloridoro and the justifications of Ipomene after Acrimante's first attempt on her virtue. In the end, a longer complication arises from Acrimante's imprisonment for this attempt (with its prison set), and from the death sentence decreed by Atrace but deflected by Atamira, who substitutes a potent narcotic for the poison intended for him; carried back to his room as a corpse, the still sleeping Acrimante is ensnared by a demon who changes the scene into the palace of Proserpina; thus he dreams of love with the goddess of hell (which leads to the dance of monsters that constitutes the *intermedio* after the second act). Once more back in his chambers, Acrimante awakens and after having terrified Bibi, who believed him dead, and rejected Atamira, who has saved his life once more, prepares a new attempt on Ipomene, which leads to the murder of Tidemo.

Some of the situations from the earlier tradition are recognizable, even in operatic disguise. Apart from those already mentioned of the shipwreck and of "the shepherdesses fishing on the seashore," ready to be courted by Acrimante, there remain also the exchange of the cloak (but in this instance it is Bibi who asks it of his master in order to cut a better figure before Delfa) and Acrimante's ridicule of the murdered Tidemo's statue:

Vieni, t'attendo;	Come, I await you.
e la mia parca mensa,	And if my frugal table
s'altro dar non ti può,	Can offer you nothing else,
cibo saran tue lacerate membra,	Your mangled limbs will be food,
tuo cadavere esangue,	Your corpse bloodless,
e beverem di tue ferite il sangue.	And we will drink the blood of your wounds.

As usual, Bibi's narration to Atamira of his master's death is comic:

Scura amena verdura,	Dark, pleasing verdure,
apparecchiata mensa	A well-dressed table
a noi si presentò;	Presented itself to us.
mangiavamo sì ben, ch'al suolo istesso	We were dining so well that the earth itself
si mosse l'appetito,	Gained an appetite.
aprì la bocca, e t'inghiottì il marito.	It opened its mouth and swallowed your husband.
Poi ti dirò la storia	Later I will tell you
del bamboccio che vola,	Of the babe who flies.
ch'or mi manca lo spirto e la parola.	For now, I lack the spirit, and words fail me.

Alessandro Melani, to whom was entrusted the task of clothing all these diffuse events with music, was the younger brother of Jacopo and had been called to Rome a little earlier in the autumn of 1667 to direct the *cappella* of Santa Maria Maggiore, an appointment that probably reflects his connections with the Rospigliosi family (he was from Pistoia and had been held at the baptismal font by a Rospigliosi related to the reigning pontiff, Clement IX). He was barely thirty years old, but had had experience in church music since he was a boy as a chorister in Pistoia and later also as *maestro di cappella* in Ferrara; however, we have only vague evidence of a single opera by him before *L'empio punito*.[27] The score of this opera, now in the Vatican Library, already shows him to be an expert, adaptable musician with a fluent pen, secure and attentive to seizing upon all the suggestions in the text that could enrich his musical discourse: alternating tuneful passages skillfully with passages of pure recitative, and occasionally interrupting arias with dramatic moments of recitative. Surely his experience as a church musician also helped him to introduce brief choral episodes as frequently as possible into an operatic tradition where they were unusual, from the chorus of stableboys in the first scene to that of demons in Acrimante's idyllic dream of Proserpina (however, it lacks the other choral episode, also infernal, that could have accompanied, before the final happy ending, the scene of Charon in his barque carrying away Acrimante's soul). He also makes free use of instruments—two parts for treble instruments, probably violins—in the opening sinfonia, in the danced intermezzi, and above all in the accompaniment to a good number of the arias; other arias and most of the recitatives are accompanied instead only by basso continuo, for which the choice of instruments (mainly chitarrone and harpsichord) was left to the performers. In all, therefore, Melani shows himself to be an up-to-date musician in Rome, which in a few years (1679) would see the beginning of Alessandro Scarlatti's operatic activity (it would have been easy for Melani to follow the operatic performances in Florence from Pistoia). And he must have had the aid of the best singers available in Rome, capable of equalling the two whom we know by name, Giuseppe Fede, soprano, and Francesco Verdoni, bass, papal singers who were permitted to absent themselves from the chapel "for the weekdays during carnival because they were occupied with the opera."[28]

The soprano Fede and some other comparable castrato probably interpreted the roles of Cloridoro and Acrimante, following the custom that had already established itself in Rome over the course of several decades. Their voices appear a little higher than the others, also for soprano, of their feminine counterparts, Ipomene and Atamira. With regard to the female roles, we do not know if the prohibition against women in Rome mounting the public stage applied during the Rospigliosi papacy; moreover, as we have already seen, it is unclear whether performances at the Teatro Colonna were considered public. Atrace, a character who is obviously more solemn and perhaps more temperate, is a bass. In the buffo couple, the servant Bibi is a bass, and the nurse Delfa is a tenor, conforming to an operatic tradition that had been established assigning to comic parts the bleating timbre of a tenor or the harsh voice of a contralto. All the choruses are for men's voices in three parts, except for the chorus of seamen in the shipwreck scene, which is in four parts; not having the means at his disposal for even a brief storm (the symphonic resources for which would not appear until Vivaldi, almost a half century later, and then not in opera), Melani must have thought of supplying it by intensifying the choral effect.

Atamira, the constant counterweight to Acrimante, is the character to whom the text and music give the greatest dramatic impetus. This is evident from the very first aria in the gentle fluency of the triple rhythm and even more in the recitative that immediately follows (see Example 1). But in more dramatic moments it is more vigorously evident in the tenser rhythm, for example in the lament that she sings a little later after being scorned and rejected by Acrimante, "Piangete, occhi, piangete" (I, v; Example 2), which begins in common time, effectively counterpointed by the violins and interrupted by a passage of recitative, and is taken up again briefly before giving way to a more extensive 3/2, which accompanies her gradual surrender to fatigue and sleep. Acrimante also has a good number of arias and diverse lyrical stances. Among others is an unusual strophic aria that immediately follows a stage direction referring to "soldiers chaining Acrimante," an aria that stands out because of the biting, insistent chordal dissonances with which the violins accompany him uninterruptedly. Acrimante sings the first strophe, "Se d'Amor la cruda sfinge / Prigioniero il cor mi tiene" ["If Love's cruel sphynx / holds my heart prisoner"] (II, ix; Example 3), and Atamira sings the second to the same music, "Crudelissime catene / ch'al mio bene il piè stringete" ["Most cruel chains / That bind the feet of my beloved"], reversing the order of the two texts in the libretto; it appears therefore that the composer was in a position to permit himself initiatives also with regard to the poet (or poets).

Acrimante expresses himself more forcefully a few scenes later when he is in prison (II, xiv). The text of his soliloquy is not among the most perspicuous, but his defiance of the powers of heaven and hell and his scorn of divine punishment nevertheless emerge already in the text:

Tormentatemi sempre	Torment me always,
con più tenaci tempre	With most tenacious tempers,
ceppi, catene e lacci,	Fetters, chains and snares,
finché disciolta sia	Until my soul is free
da gl'amorosi impacci,	From love's entanglements
e dal misero sen l'anima mia.	And from my wretched breast.
Su, dileguatevi	Rise up, vanish,
larve d'amor,	Specters of love,
su, separatevi	Rise up, separate,
spirti dal cor.	O spirits from my heart.
Poich'a duello eterno	For an eternal duel
doppo la morte mia sfido l'inferno,	I offer hell after my death,
e doppo aver lo sdegno	And after venting my disdain

seco sfogato, e col tartareo regno	Against hell, and joined
il mio valor congiunto,	The realm of Tartarus with my valor,
moverò cruda guerra al Re dell'Etra,	I will wage cruel war against the king of heaven,
del cui poter mi rido,	Whose power I laugh at,
se punir non mi fa da un uom di pietra	If he does not punish me with a man of stone.

The musical rendering is varied and concise and shows how unconstrained and energetic the fluidity of seventeenth-century opera was, far from the rigid contrast between aria and recitative that would prevail in the following century. It opens (Example 4) with a vigorous phrase without melodic repetitions that corresponds to the first six verses, which are framed by two ritornellos played by the violins; to evoke the "ghosts of love" it softens and melts, passing from duple meter to a more languid 3/2; but it quickly returns, though with different accents, to the warlike passages of the beginning for defying hell; and finally bursts forth into a vigorous recitative when it arrives at the blasphemous challenge, "Re dell'Etra," underlining with a melodic leap the foreboding of punishment that will come from the "man of stone," a recurrent characteristic of all of the various *Convitati di pietra*.

The part of Bibi is diffuse. He is employed in part as counterpoint to his master, in part entangled in the acidulous comic situations of his courting Delfa. Another servant who plays a minor role addresses epithets like "toothless old hag," and "ugly old witch" to Delfa; Bibi also often waxes ironic about her presumed beauties, and when she wants to come to the point ("tutto va ben, ma non intendo come / possa ferir per via di sguardi un ceco" ["Everything is fine, but I do not understand how / I can strike a blind man through my gazes"]), he responds equivocally:

Ciuco son io, che ti mirai con l'occhio	I am an ass, since I looked at you with
del core, e non del viso,	My heart's and not my head's eye,
e di veder mi parve	And I thought I saw paradise
nel tuo volto d'inferno il paradiso.	In your hellish face.

But he still flatters her, a little for his own sake, a little to use her as a means to realize Acrimante's designs on Ipomene. Bibi sings bass, and it was a part of the operatic tradition of his day that bass voices usually doubled the part of the basso continuo; since the humor, rather than depending on a particular melodic style, was above all entrusted to the perspicuity of the impudent and at times salacious text, to charged enunciation and sly mimicry, talents that the dwarf who played the role in 1669 certainly possessed.[29] A brief tenor arietta for Delfa serves to give an idea of Melani's comic manner, which assumes the incisive characteristics of a rapid syllabic style (II, i; Example 5).

The lovers Ipomene and Cloridoro dialogue close at hand or make love to each other from afar in happy duets and in suave arias that already provide a foretaste of bel canto; they reprove each other in scenes of jealousy with bitterly accented recitatives. For the sake of brevity, it suffices to give a taste of the former with a short aria of Cloridoro's (II, xix; Example 6). Let us turn rather to one of the most successful moments in the opera, one that reinforces Acciaiuoli's spectacular marvels (II, ix): the scene of the enticing dream that the demon offers Acrimante. In the score, it is entitled "Introduzione al ballo" because it introduces the dance of the infernal monsters (in the score this is entitled "Ballo delle furie"), which will provide the *intermedio* between the acts. The demon introduces it with a varied, vigorous recitative:

Or che sopito giace	Now that he has been lulled to sleep,
il mio fedele amico	My faithful friend,
con astuzia mendace	With mendacious cunning
assicurar vogl'io	I want to make sure
sopra l'anima sua l'impero mio.	Of my dominion over his soul.
Porrò con finto inganno	With the feigned deceptions
di sogno, e visione	Of dreams and visions I will compare
alle gioie del mondo	The delights of the abyss
i diletti d'abisso in paragone;	To the joys of the world.
e a sodisfar le sue sfrenate voglie	And to satisfy his unbridled desire
d'amorosi trofei,	For love trophies,
apparir li farò ne i regni miei	I will have appear before him here in my realm
beltà divina al suo voler soggetta,	Divine beauty in his thrall,
e per danze, e tornei	And with dances and tourneys,
turba gentile a i suoi piaceri eletta.	A host of gentle folk chosen for his delight.

Here, through the miracle of theatrical engineering, "the scene is changed into the palace of Proserpina, where Proserpina is discovered on her throne surrounded by many monsters and spirits; Acrimante rests on a rug in the same palace." The enticing invitations of the goddess alternate with the brief responses of the dreaming Acrimante, sometimes in recitative, sometimes in arioso, these passages always crowned with an elaborate "Chorus of Demons" exhorting "Ai diletti, alle gioie" ["To delight, to joy"]. At the climax is the duet between Proserpina and the demon, "Del regno d'Erebo / tremendi sudditi, / del fiero Cerbero / latrati orribili, /sonate, / cantate" ["Dread subjects / Of the realm of Erebus, / Cerberus' / Horrible barking, / Resound, / Sing out"]. (Example 7), which shows how Melani's invention exploits the force and variety of his melodic and instrumental resources. In a different way, this is also confirmed by the ballet that follows, in which the formal symmetry demanded by the repetitions of the dance is brought to life by changes in tempo: Adagio, Allegro, and finally Presto.

The story continues along its usual course with the scene in "Tidemo's garden [not in a graveyard] with his statue and those of others" and with a single dinner, for which Acrimante, the blasphemer, asks of Pluto that he prepare a table:

A te ricorro, o Pluto,	I turn to you, o Pluto,
e di tanto favore	And for such a favor
sarà l'anima mia prezzo dovuto!	My soul will be the price!
Ad onta delle stelle a me concedi	In defiance of the stars, grant me
una mensa gradita, acciò ch'io possa	A well-prepared table, so that I can keep
conservar la parola a chi la diedi.	My word to the person I gave it.
Furie, demoni, aita,	Furies, demons, help.
se d'essermi crudel ha il ciel prefisso,	If heaven has reckoned to be cruel to me,
spero trovar pietoso almen l'abisso.	I hope to find the abyss merciful.

Thus is placed in motion Acciaiuoli's theatrical genius, through which "appear six real statues with a table already set." Another variant has Bibi, in spite of himself, giving his hand to Tidemo's statue in order to help him to sit down at the table; and Tidemo, unexpectedly loquacious, with his last words justifies the miracle of his flight:

L'alma donasti a Pluto, a lui la rendi,	You gave your soul to Pluto, render it to him.
e per mia gloria, e tuo tormento eterno,	And for my glory and your eternal torment,
mentr'io men volo al Ciel, scendi all'inferno.	While I fly to heaven, descend to hell.

The conclusion is delayed by other scenic wonders by Acciaiuoli: first the statue moves once again to terrify Bibi, then, once the infernal scene has appeared, the encounter between "Charon in his barque and Acrimante" takes place. Returned to earth, Bibi first announces Acrimante's disappearance to Atamira, then asks for and receives consolation in a long duet with Delfa. Surprisingly, Atamira is placid:

E qual placida calma	What placid calm
sento nel mio pensier? Folle vaneggio:	Pervades my mind? I must be mad:
perdo il consorte, e godo?	I lose my husband and am happy?
Perdei il consorte, è ver, ma a nuove nozze	I have lost my husband, it is true; but to another wedding
il Cielo or mi richiama:	Heaven now calls me.
perdei chi m'odia, acquisterò chi m'ama.	I lost someone who hated me; I acquire someone who loves me.

Thus everything is ready for the last scene, before which she informs Atrace of all that has happened, including her change of heart; and thus slowly navigating arrives the end of this seventeenth-century antecedent to Mozart's opera, after the manner of operas, with the wedding of Atamira to Atrace (which averts a war between Macedonia and Corinth) and of Ipomene to Cloridoro. All four rejoice, and to Bibi's question, "E il mio caro padron chi me lo rende?" ["And who will give me back my dear master?"], they respond in concordant voices with the moral, which justifies the title: "Così punisce il Ciel, chi il Cielo offende" ["Thus heaven punishes him who offends heaven"].

CHAPTER TWO: THE EIGHTEENTH CENTURY

1. Arcadia and Reform of the Opera Libretto:
Opera Seria and Comic Opera

At the beginning of the eighteenth century, the Arcadian academy, which had been founded in Rome in 1689 to carry on the cultural program of the circle that had surrounded Queen Christina of Sweden, was already bringing together in Rome and its numerous colonies throughout Italy most of the men who in one way or another considered themselves literati. For many, becoming an Arcadian shepherd was primarily a matter of prestige and a pleasant social diversion; but the best Arcadians seriously discussed poetry and problems of criticism, and, even without a well-defined program, professed an intent "to restore Italian poetry, which had been thrown into confusion through the barbarities of the last century, to exterminate bad taste and to insure that it never resurface." The Arcadians were largely unsympathetic toward music, even though Bernardo Pasquini, Alessandro Scarlatti, and Arcangelo Corelli were admitted to the Roman group; Lodovico Antonio

Muratori, one of the most severe critics of the seventeenth century, laid the blame for the corruption of theater and the abandonment of tragedy on opera, which was the principal representative of "modern" music for the Arcadians:

> Today the noblest, sweetest, not to say only, entertainment and solace of citizens is to hear a drama recited, i.e., sung, by musicians. As people have become used to the taste of this dish and lost the taste for other theatrical works, comedy has become the prey of performers who know nothing other than how to make people laugh [i.e., actors of the commedia dell'arte], if not with obscene witticisms, then with dishonest lies, and stupid, ridiculous, shameful inventions. Tragedy also, because it is dressed in too much severity and not pleasing to the ears through musical means, is abhorred . . . . For these reasons worthy poets were and still are constrained to weave *drammi musicali* if they wish to appear with their verse in the theater; having no other means of hoping to please the people.[1]

And elsewhere:

> The overwhelming popularity of these modern dramas is of little profit, and may cause great damage to the well-regulated city . . . as is well known to the best poets in Italy; but in order to serve the taste of the times, poets suffer this forced ignorance, not wishing to wear out their brains composing true tragedies and comedies, which perhaps might find neither actors to present them nor audiences that would willingly listen to them.[2]

Certainly, Muratori would have placed among the "worthy poets" constrained by "this forced ignorance" Apostolo Zeno (1668–1750), who became a librettist in order to earn a livelihood, but whose vocation was that of erudite antiquarian.[3] Zeno had once written Muratori (in 1701) that it was impossible to write opera libretti according to the good rules of the art of drama and also succeed with the public: "The more one wants to keep to the rules, the more one displeases, and if the libretto receives some praise, it enjoys but a small audience. In this, the music is much at fault, since through the weak understanding of composers the best scenes are weakened; and much at fault are the singers who do not even know how to act out the scenes."[4] With these criticisms of composers and singers Zeno anticipates *Il teatro alla moda* (Venice, 1720) by the patrician composer Benedetto Marcello (who, however, did not write opera), that most famous and amusing libel in which the entire operatic world is held up to ridicule with ironic advice to its components: the librettists, composers, singers, and so forth, down to the supernumeraries and machinists, and even the patrons and mothers of the divas.[5]

Various Arcadian poets applied themselves to the reform of the operatic libretto, including Silvio Stampiglia, Domenico David, Girolamo Frigimelica Roberti, and Pietro Pariati; but the greatest merit was later attributed to Zeno through the authority he derived from having held the post of *poeta cesareo* in Vienna, from 1710 to 1731, with the responsibility of writing texts in various genres of musical drama, including opera, which was the delight of the imperial court.[6] The reformers did not have a well-defined program, beyond that of simplifying and purifying poetic language, restoring the opera libretto to the tragic genre in some way, and restoring the reputation of tragedy, including tragedy that "delights the ear through music." Several libretti adopted the subtitle *Tragedia per musica* and the classical division into five acts, which they quickly had to renounce because of the practical and economic difficulties arising from the larger number of intervals between the acts and of the corresponding intermezzi.[7] They also introduced more elegant management of the action and the so-called *liaison des scènes* (having before them the example of French tragedy, which would later form the model for Metastasian opera too); they agreed in their preference for strong and noble sentiments and loves, and they wanted to render the psychology of the characters more coherently. But in the end the most tangible and permanent result was the elimination from opera of comic characters and the scenes in which they develop their particular subplots (we have seen an example in *L'empio punito* by Acciaiuoli and Melani). Thus was born the genre to which the label *opera seria* is usually applied, clearly distinct from the various genres in which the comic elements soon reappeared. The latter is designated with the generic label of *opera comica*, or—in my opinion less appropriately—*opera buffa*.

In 1731, Zeno was succeeded as *poeta cesareo* by Pietro Trapassi, i.e., Metastasio (1698–1782), also a member of Arcadia, where he went under the name "Artino Corasio." Metastasio possessed greater literary, if not dramatic, talent. After distinguishing himself as a librettist in Naples, Rome, and Venice, he held his post at the Viennese court until his death and was for more than half a century the dominant figure among librettists of *opera seria*.[8] After being set to music by the composers of the court in Vienna, his libretti, more often than those of other poets, Zeno included, were set by numerous other composers and staged throughout Europe.[9] The high point was reached with *Artaserse*, written already during his Italian period and set to music between 1730 and 1785 by no fewer that eighty composers; but *Alessandro nelle Indie*, *Didone abbandonata*, and *Adriano in Siria* were not far behind. Yet, despite such extraordinary successes, *opera seria* was still considered by some an artificial and unnatural genre,[10] so that over the course of the century criticisms, polemics, and more or less radical attempts at reform arose once again from several sides.

The consideration of these latter do not enter into the theme that I intend to treat here. It will, however, be useful to note that if the reform attributed to Zeno improved the literary quality of opera libretti, it did not correct the abuses of singers and composers he had ventured to criticize.[11] To the contrary, the length of the dialogues and monologues that carried the development of the dramatic situations forward, but that were destined to be treated for the most part with the most schematic declamation supported by chords in the harpsichord (secco recitative), favored the tendency toward the so-called opera-concerto—a series of arias tenuously linked by the thread of the dramatic action to which the greater part of the public paid little attention. The fact that audiences often heard the same libretti several times, even though with different singers and different music, also contributed to this; the well-known circumstances of the action permitted members of the audience to divert themselves during the long recitatives and to concentrate their attention on the arias (whose texts were often changed).[12]

One immediate result of the Arcadian critiques was the expunction of comic elements and characters from operatic plots; they reappeared beginning in the first decade of the eighteenth century in action independent of the main stage work and with the function of intermezzi between the acts—a function that hitherto had been entrusted to ballets. In Venice, the first intermezzi of this type were staged in 1706 at the Teatro San Cassiano and Teatro Sant'Angelo, which provide us with the first printed libretti of intermezzi;[13] but quickly the practice spread and led to a genre that enjoyed great success during the entire first half of the century. The normal division of an opera into three acts (I have already mentioned that libretti in five acts failed to gain ground) usually required two intermezzi, three only if one wanted to add another after the third act; very soon the tendency prevailed of extracting the two episodes as parts of a comic action of its own, usually entrusted to two characters (soprano and bass) along with a mute character. A famous example, though a little later, is *La serva padrona* [The Maid as Mistress] by Giovambattista Pergolesi (1710–1736), staged for the first time in Naples in 1733 between the acts of *Il prigioniero superbo* [The Proud Prisoner], an *opera seria* by the same composer. With time, the intermezzi gained a larger number of characters and episodes and were often divorced from the original function expressed by their label; performed as productions of their own, they became one among the various forms of comic opera, distinguishing themselves only through their more modest proportions. Around 1750, they were once again supplanted by ballets in their function of designating act divisions.

Comic opera, which during the eighteenth century took its place beside *opera seria*, distinguishing itself clearly as a genre in its own right, was not completely new. Already in the seventeenth century there were examples, though not often, of operas with plots that were substantially comic. Such were, for example, those already mentioned by Giovanni Andrea Moniglia, *Il podestà di Colognole* [The Mayor of Colognole] (1656), *Il vecchio balordo* [The Old Fool] (1658), *Tacere e amare* [To Keep Silent and Love] (1674), labelled *drammi civili* and thus retaining the classical distinction whereby comedy consisted in the actions of private citizens, tragedy in those of noble or royal characters. We can add to this list *Il Trespolo tutore* [Trespolo the Tutor] by Giovanni Cosimo Villifranchi (after G.B. Ricciardi), with music by Alessandro Stradella (Genoa, 1679), *Tutto il male non vien per nuocere* [It's an Ill Wind that Blows Nobody Any Good] by Giuseppe D. de Totis and Alessandro Scarlatti (Rome, 1681; Florence, 1686; Naples, 1687), *Gli amori alla moda* [Fashionable Loves], *scherzo melodrammatico* with music by G.B. Bassani (Ferrara, 1688), and *Gl'inganni amorosi scoperti in villa* [Love Illusions Revealed], *scherzo giocoso* with music by Giuseppe Aldrovandini (Bologna, 1696). It is nevertheless remarkable that in 1709 the Teatro dei Fiorentini in

Naples began an intensive activity dedicated exclusively to comic operas, for the most part in Neapolitan dialect, with *Patro' Calienno de la Costa*, "commeddia pe museca de lo Dottore Agasippo Mercotellis, posta 'n museca da lo segnore Antinicco Arefice" (i.e., *commedia per musica* by Dr. A. Mercotellis, set to music by Antonino Orefice). Among the composers, some of whom are little known, Orefice, who was one of the most active, also composed *opere serie* for the larger Neapolitan opera house; in 1718 Alessandro Scarlatti's *Il trionfo dell'onore* [The Triumph of Honor] also appeared at the Teatro dei Fiorentini; and in 1719 Leonardo Vinci (1696–1730) made his debut with *Lo cecato fauso*, the first of a series of musical comedies whose scores have been lost; the autograph score for *Li zite 'n galera* [The Loves on the Galley] of 1722, however, does survive. Vinci would soon have successes also in Rome and Venice as one of the most highly prized masters of *opera seria*.

The Neapolitan example had almost immediate repercussions in Venice with *Elisa* (libretto by Domenico Lalli and music by Giovanni M. Ruggieri), *commedia da rappresentarsi per musica,* in 1711 at the Teatro Sant'Angelo. But it was not until 1717 that the Teatro San Fantino staged *L'ambizione castigata* [Ambition Castigated], *comidrama in musica* (libretto by Francesco Mazzari, music by various unspecified composers), and *Bertoldo*, *drama tragicomico* (libretto by Francesco Passerini, music by Girolamo Bassani), followed in 1718 by *Il vecchio deluso* [The Deluded Old Man], *drama comico musicale*, and by *La figlia che canta* [The Singing Daughter], *divertimento comico musicale* (libretti by Francesco Passerini; the music of the first unknown; the music of the second by Carlo Francesco Pollarolo).[14] Almost at the same time, in 1718, the Bolognese Giuseppe Maria Buini (1687–1739) began his continuous activity as a composer with two comic operas presented at the Teatro Formagliari in Bologna, *L'ipocondriaco* [The Hypochondriac] (libretto by Giovanni Cosimo Villifranchi) and *Il mago deluso* [The Sorcerer Deceived] (libretto by Antonio Zaniboni). It is not without significance that after debuting in the comic genre he should seek to confirm his success in Venice with *opere serie*, and would only return to comic opera later (to his own libretti) with a series of works: *Il savio delirante* [The Delirious Wise Man] (1726); *Albumazar* (1727); *Malmocor* (1728, but restaged in 1731 with the title *Artaganamenone, tragichissimissimo dramma per musica*); *Chi non fa non falla* [Nothing Ventured, Nothing Failed] (1729); *I diporti d'amore in villa* [Love Pleasures in the Country] (1729); *Fidarsi è bene, ma non fidari è meglio* [To Trust Is Good, Not To Trust Is Better] (1731); *L'ortolana contessa* [The Gardener Countess] (1732); *La Zanina maga per amore* [Zanina, Sorceress for the Sake of Love] (1737). Like the comic operas by Giuseppe Aldrovandini from the end of the seventeenth century, as well as those performed in Naples at the Teatro dei Fiorentini, Buini's works also are often in dialect. This fact, however, limited the possibilities of the same opera being presented in other cities, so that soon dialect was avoided or limited to the roles of caricatures, the *buffi caricati*, of which I shall say more below.

All in all, it is clear that the prestige musical theater had gained in the course of more than a century had been inherited above all by *opera seria*, if for no other reason than the fact that the most famous singers and those most admired by the public, especially the castrati, were best suited to serious roles; while the comic roles traditionally were entrusted instead to singers who were less gifted vocally but self-possessed and versatile on the stage. There was a tendency to attribute less importance to comic performances as social events; they were welcomed more readily in provincial theaters, while in larger cities, especially in Venice, they were only given intermittently, in theaters of minor importance, and in seasons of more popular character.[15]

In contrast, in Naples performances of comic operas at the Teatro dei Fiorentini had a degree of continuity and were soon emulated in other theaters like the Teatro Nuovo and the Teatro della Pace, while *opera seria* continued to be reserved for the Teatro San Bartolomeo, which from 1737 was replaced by the grandiose, new Teatro San Carlo. In this context, there was a tendency to accord the two genres almost equal consideration; composers issuing forth from the four Neapolitan conservatories readily produced works in both genres, and their success in this period in the field of *opera seria* in Italy and abroad favored the diffusion of their comic operas from one end of Europe to the other (aside from the above-mentioned Vinci and Pergolesi, worth citing are the careers of Leonardo Leo, Pietro Auletta, Rinaldo da Capua, Gaetano Latilla, Nicolò Logroscino, Nicolò Jommelli, Tommaso Traetta, Nicolò Piccinni, Giovanni Paisiello, and Domenico Cimarosa). After 1740, the number of performances of comic operas increased remarkably in Venice also; toward the middle of the century, almost half the operas performed in its various theaters belonged to the comic genre, and only the Teatro San Giovanni Grisostomo (which was later superseded by the Teatro San Benedetto) continued to give *opere serie* exclusively (with comic intermezzi between the acts).[16] This favored the rapprochement between *opera seria* and comic opera even by non-Neapolitan composers, among whom Baldassare Galuppi (1706–1785) is particularly remembered, both for his gifts as a musician and for the fact that his comic operas often used libretti by Carlo Goldoni.

Thus far I have spoken of comic opera, expressly avoiding the other frequently used term *opera buffa*, which I consider improper and apt to create misunderstandings, especially for those who do not speak Italian. I consider it improper because, contrary to general opinion, very rarely does it appear in eighteenth-century libretti. To be sure, it must have been part of theatrical jargon, since Mozart himself applies it at one point to his own *Don Giovanni*;[17] but in Wiel's catalogue of operas produced in Venice during the eighteenth century, only five bear the subtitle *opera buffa* out of a total of about 1300 titles (in my opinion, these five instances reflect the personal preference of a single librettist, Carlo Lanfranchi Rossi).[18] More typically, the term *buffo* is instead found in the dramatis personae. The first instance is in *Il protettore alla moda* [The Fashionable Patron], *dramma giocoso per musica* (a reworking of a text by Buini, reset to music by Galuppi for the Teatro San Cassiano in 1747; the libretto for the 1749 restaging labels the work a *dramma comico per musica*), which lists three *parti serie* and four *parti buffe*; but more common is a distribution of two *parti serie* and five *parti buffe* (as in the commedia dell'arte, the *parti serie* are usually two lovers). Later, with *Il Conte Caramella* by Goldoni and Galuppi (1751), begins a greater variety of distinguishing qualifiers, which include, beyond the *parti serie*, roles of *mezzo carattere* (sometimes called *buffi di mezzo carattere*) and *buffi caricati*.

It seems to me that the term *opera buffa* should also be avoided because it suggests an insistent prevalence of farcical or even scurrilous effects. Though it cannot be denied that many comic operas are not all that subtle, it should be kept in mind that they had a variety of means to invite laughter. There were pastorals (usually labelled *drama comico pastorale* or *divertimento comico pastorale*); there were heroico-comic operas inspired by well-known literary characters like Orlando or Don Quixote; there were mythological comedies and caricatures of tragedies, like *Urganostocor*, for example;[19] there were satires of the world of the theater, the earliest being the intermezzo *La Dirindina* by Girolamo Gigli and Domenico Scarlatti, which was staged in Rome in 1715; there was local color, underlined by the use of dialect in the Neapolitan *commedie pe' museca* or the Bolognese operas by Buini; there was, finally, that which is typical of every comedy, the more or less successful attempt to present the common people, their good and bad qualities, their weaknesses, in contrast to the dignified but often unreal comportment of the heroes and heroines of *opera seria*. The duets and retaliations of lovers and the pathetic accents already present in the oldest intermezzi, like Pergolesi's *Serva padrona*, provide variety and contrast within particular operas; not to speak of the vogue beginning in the middle of the century for operas inspired by the model of the *comédie larmoyante*.

Having traced, even in summary fashion, the serious and comic operatic scene of the eighteenth century, I must, before coming to speak of new *Convitati di pietra*, make two excursions into the field of spoken theater and ballet, to mention other theatrical events inspired by our theme in contexts distinct from opera. Nevertheless these excursions are suggested by the influence that such events had on events more specifically connected to my main theme.

2. Don Giovanni in Arcadia

The typically baroque substance of the myth of Don Giovanni could not easily be reconciled with the directions of thought and taste and with the spirit of reform that made itself felt at the beginning of the eighteenth century. For the entire century, there was in fact but one new literary elaboration.[20] This single exception was inspired with the intention of reform, *Don Giovanni Tenorio, o sia Il dissoluto*, one of Carlo Goldoni's first theatrical works, with which in 1736 he attempted to purify and make the old plot more verisimilitudinous in order to reconcile it with the literary taste of his day. We should not believe that the character disappeared from the commedia dell'arte repertoire; Goldoni himself is witness to the fact that he continued to appear with all the characteristics and excesses consecrated by tradition. In the preface to his work, Goldoni cites with disdain "*Il convitato di pietra*, most fortunate comedy by Don Pedro Calderon della Barca [sic], full of defects and improprieties as it is, and as one still sees it performed by Italian actors"; he laments that "for many years now, no work has experienced such continuous popular applause in the theater as has this work." It is well known that throughout his career Goldoni (1707–1793) made his main goal that of opposing the traditional buffoonery and the equivocal and lubricious comedy of the "improvised" performance with regular comedy, as he conceived it, well-mannered and well supervised. The vicissitudes of his battle had their ups and downs, however, and his successes did not prevent the old practices of the commedia dell'arte from continuing to gain applause almost through to the end of the century. When it came to an end, it was, more than any other reason, because of the hostility of governmental authorities toward a genre that eluded the censor's control all too easily.

Goldoni was himself also an Arcadian and the substance of his campaign was clearly related to the action promoted from the beginning of the century by the academy to which he belonged under the name "Polisseno Fegejo." He also, before turning with more felicitous results to comic activity, was tempted by the mirage of a restoration of dramatic theater, to which end seem directed several tragicomedies in hendecasyllabic verse.[21] Written between 1732 and 1739, they were intended for performance without music, however close in intent and literary style to the *drammi musicali* of Zeno and Metastasio.[22] This group includes *Don Giovanni Tenorio*, in which Goldoni clearly shows his intention of focusing on the protagonist by choosing his name as the main title, as had Molière. His minute exposition of the absurdities of the old story in his preface also serves as a list of all that he wanted to eliminate:

> A man . . . is received by a noble lady in the dark; she welcomes him into her arms instead of another and is only aware of the deception when he tries to escape. At these querulous voices . . . appears the King of Naples with candle in hand; Don Giovanni puts out the light of the candle with his sword. . . . Discovered, . . . he departs for Castile; a storm casts him into the sea, and fortune throws him up upon the shore, in his powdered wig, and his feet do not even seem to have gotten wet. I will not speak of the servant . . . with whom he exchanges gratuitous improprieties, villainies and kicks . . . ; each scene has its portion of absurdities and improprieties. Sufficing for all the others is the marble statue erected in a few minutes, that walks, goes to dinner, invites to dinner, threatens, avenges itself, and performs miracles; to crown the work,[23] all the listeners pass safe and sound along with the protagonist to the devil's abode.[24]

The most notable expunction, and more in accord with the ideas of Zeno, is that of Don Giovanni's servant and companion to his adventures, a character that was so important in Tirso and Molière and even predominating in the "improvised" performances of the commedia dell'arte. The comic figures of the shepherdess Elisa and her lover Carino compensate, but they are of an attenuated comedy and rusticity, in conformity with the style of the *pastorale per musica* that reformers who followed Zeno practiced as an alternative to opera with historical or mythological subject matter. The clear literary derivation of one of Elisa's monologues suffices to show her attenuated comic status:[25]

È tempo omai che una costante fiamma	It is high time that a constant flame
Nel mio seno s'accenda. Amai finora	Should be lit in my breast. 'Til this point,
Quasi per giuoco, or vo' cambiar costume.	I loved almost as a game; now I want to change.
Di Titiro e Montan, d'Ergasto e Silvio,	With Titiro and Montan, Ergasto and Silvio,
Di Licisca e Megacle e di Fileno,	Licisca, Megacle, Fileno,
E di tant'altri che mi furo amanti,	And all the others who were my lovers,
Finsi gradir per vanità l'affetto;	I feigned to gratify their love out of vanity.
Carino ha un non so che fuor dell'usato,	Carino has a certain something out of the ordinary
Che mi penetra il cuor. . . .	That pierces my heart. . . .

That certain something of Carino's does not prevent Elisa from welcoming, a few minutes later, out of vanity and ambition to change her station, the attentions of the fair cavalier, who reaches her unaccompanied, since an assault by robbers has caused his servants to flee. Even though "despoiled of his clothes," he has sufficient prestige to flatter her; so they approach her cabin, leaving the way clear for the customary robbers (who in one stroke have eliminated the traditional shipwreck, the powdered wig and any equivalent of Catalinón or Sganarelle) to assault Donna Isabella, a Neapolitan woman in men's clothes, directly afterward. Duke Ottavio intervenes to rescue her, and she immediately confides to him that she is in search of Don Giovanni, the fiancé (also Neapolitan) who seduced and abandoned her. In Act II, in which all this happens, we see Don Giovanni once more: "in rustic habit," he takes leave of Elisa with false promises, and Elisa using her feminine wiles makes up with Carino who has spied on them unseen.

Act II is pastoral and has as its stage setting "the countryside near [!] Castile"; but the rest of the action takes place at court, with conflicts of loves and hates typical of Metastasio. In Act I, Donna Anna unhappily received the announcement that the King of Castile intends her for his nephew, Duke Ottavio, whom she hates (for an instant she deludes herself that the king himself wants to marry her). In Act III, the announcement is received with the same ill will by Ottavio, and the meeting between the two gives Donna Anna the opportunity to insinuate that Ottavio has a lover at court (Isabella, for whom he indeed is beginning to harbor tender feelings). Isabella is in search of Don Giovanni, finds him at court, is spurned by him, and seeks vengeance in a duel; the others begin to nurture doubts about Don Giovanni, but he counters by giving them to believe that Isabella is mad.

In Act IV, the Commendatore, Donna Anna's father, has invited Don Giovanni, whom he met in Naples, to dinner. Dinner over, it is announced that the king's minister desires to speak with the Commendatore; Donna Anna remains alone with Don Giovanni and is curious about his glances toward her during dinner, but she proudly opposes his violent assault. The Commendatore intervenes and is killed. The minister assigns Duke Ottavio the task of arresting Don Giovanni, but the latter has taken refuge on consecrated ground where he cannot be arrested. In Act V, we find him in a "hall with various tombs, among which is the statue of the Commendatore."[26] Elisa claims she knows a way for him to escape, and he renews his promises of matrimony; but Isabella's arrival prevents his flight. In vain, Don Giovanni tries to present her as mad and to threaten her with his sword; his flight is no longer possible because of the arrival of the king's minister who threatens punishment, even though he does not yet have the power to arrest him. In another vain attempt, Don Giovanni offers to marry Donna Anna, who is in mourning. In the end, he is alone, raging and starving, surrounded in his refuge by guards; while Don Giovanni rejects the comforting remarks of Carino, "a lightning bolt strikes [him], [and] the earth opens to swallow him. . . ." It falls to Carino to narrate to Don Giovanni's persecutors, who suddenly reappear, what happened. Donna Anna remains in the background; but the death of Don Giovanni has opened the way for a future marriage between Ottavio and Isabella. Elisa tries in vain to reconcile with Carino; to her also implicitly applies the moral espoused in the final verses by the minister of the King of Castile: "Just heaven punishes the evil and abhors the dissolute."

The affinity that we have noted between *Don Giovanni Tenorio* and *dramma musicale* is confirmed in the dedication (to Michele Grimani, owner of both the Teatro San Samuele, where commedia dell'arte actors performed, and the Teatro San Giovanni Grisostomo, the temple of *opera seria*), a dedication in which the "delightful Metastasio" is mentioned once again. This does not indicate, however, that the theme could form the basis for an *opera seria*, but only confirms that Metastasian opera formed the best model Italian dramatic literature could turn to. Again in the reformed version of Don Giovanni by Goldoni, deprived of the more obvious comic characteristics, the story still preserves a rhythmic acceleration, a continual thrusting forward that would be difficult to reconcile with the comportment and tone of an *opera seria*. They will find release in the ascendency of comic opera.[26]

3. Don Giovanni in Ballet

My second excursus brings us to *Le Festin de pierre*, "ballet pantomime Composé par Mr. ANGIOLINI." Thus the program printed for the first performance at the Burgtheater in Vienna (17 October 1761); but in reality the Florentine dancer Gasparo Angiolini (1731–1803), whose name is given such typographical prominence, had composed only the plot and choreography of the ballet; the music was by Christoph Willibald Gluck (1714–1787), the composer who barely a year later would begin the most important reform of *opera seria* in the eighteenth century.

Angiolini was also an innovator in his field, creating with *Le Festin de pierre* the first *ballet d'action*, in which—as he wrote later, polemicizing over his primacy with the Frenchman Jean-Georges Noverre—he had found "without aid and without example the flourishing and interesting way to conduct through pantomime a comedy, a drama . . . an entire tragedy."[28] In fact, the program for *Le festin de pierre* (probably written by Ranieri de' Calzabigi, the librettist who was Gluck's valued collaborator in the reform of opera) is a true manifesto of Angiolini's innovations, justified from the very beginning with antiquarian considerations: "The spectacle that I present to the public is a ballet-pantomime in the style of the ancients."[29] The pretensions toward classical restoration recede into the background when it comes to discussing the action of the ballet: "I have chosen for my essay a Spanish tragicomedy that has received the approbation of all nations. . . . The unities of time and of place are not observed here, but the invention is sublime, the catastrophe terrifying and, in our opinion, verisimilitudinous";[30] and further on: "the subject is gloomy, I confess, but are perhaps those of most tragedies laughing and gay? . . . Is it perhaps forbidden to terrify with dance unlike with speech?" The ballet thus places particular emphasis on the tragic aspects of the story, the killing of the Commendatore and the final punishment of Don Giovanni. This is confirmed by the comments of the diarist Count Johann Karl von Zinzendorf, who attended several performances and noted (17 October 1761): "At the theater, they performed *Le*

Joueur and afterward the pantomime ballet *Le Festin de pierre*. The subject is extremely sad, lugubrious and terrifying"; and again (8 February 1762): "there followed *Le Festin de pierre*. There is something striking and lugubrious in the scene in which the ghost preaches to him and shows him heaven."[31]

Angiolini narrates the plot of *Le Festin de pierre* as follows:

I have divided the ballet into three acts. The first represents a public road. The house of the Commendatore is on one side, that of Don Giovanni on the other. The action begins with a serenade that Don Giovanni plays for his lover, Donna Elvira, the Commendatore's daughter. He obtains access to the house where he is surprised by the Commendatore. He fights with him; the Commendatore is killed and carried away. In the second act, Don Giovanni gives a great banquet in his house, preceded by a dance, for his friends and their lovers. After having danced they sit down to eat. At the height of their merrymaking, the Commendatore's statue knocks roughly at the door. They go to open; he enters the room; the guests are terrified and flee. Don Giovanni remains alone with the statue. He ridicules him by inviting him to eat. The statue refuses and in turn invites Don Giovanni to dine at his tomb. Don Giovanni accepts and accompanies the Commendatore to the door. The noise ceases; the guests, somewhat reassured, return to the room, but fear accompanies them, providing the occasion for an entrée of dancers all atremble. Don Giovanni returns and tries to reassure them; they abandon him. He remains alone with his servant; he gives him orders and leaves. The third act unfolds in a place destined for the interment of persons of distinction. The Commendatore's mausoleum, finished a short while ago, is in the center; he himself stands in front of his own tomb. Don Giovanni is a bit surprised to see him. However, he assumes an air of self-assurance and approaches the Commendatore. The latter takes him by the arm and exhorts him to change his way of life; but Don Giovanni appears obstinate, and despite the Commendatore's threats and the marvels he witnesses, Don Giovanni persists in his impenitence. Then the center of the earth opens, vomiting flames. From this volcano issue forth ghosts and furies who torment Don Giovanni. He is enchained by them, and in his hor-rid desperation is swallowed along with all the monsters; an earthquake covers the place with a pile of ruins.[32]

Two versions of Gluck's score survive, one short, the other near-ly twice as long; but only the first corresponds to the program of the first performance with any precision, while the second must correspond to later performances enriched with new episodes.[33] In the short version, the pieces that follow the overture correspond to the narration of the danced action as follows:

Act I
no. 1: Entrée of Don Giovanni and the musicians
no. 2: Serenade
no. 5: Duel and murder of the Commendatore;
   Don Giovanni's indifference

Act II
no. 18: Don Giovanni gallant and arrogant
no. 19: A Spanish *chacona* is danced
no. 21:Pas de deux for Don Giovanni and a lady
no. 22: *Danse générale*
no. 23: Knocks at the door; fear of the person who goes to open it;
   entrance of the statue; the guests flee
no. 24: Don Giovanni is alone with the statue
no. 25: The guests enter fearfully; despite Don Giovanni's assurances
   (return of the theme of no. 18), they flee once again in fear
no. 26: Don Giovanni remains alone with his servant

Act III
no. 30: Don Giovanni and the statue in the graveyard
no. 31: A fiery abyss opens; dance of specters and furies;
   Don Giovanni descends into the earth

In the longer version, two pieces (nos. 3-4) evidently fill out Act I; Act II receives four pieces (nos. 20 and 27-29; but the last is a repeat of no. 26); Act III is unchanged. The largest addition, nos. 6-17, must form an entirely new episode or act, but it is unclear how any of these additions correspond to the danced action.[34] The performance of the original version in 1761 is not supposed to have lasted more than twenty minutes, a brevity understandable, both because this is the first experiment in *ballet d'action*, and because a simple, concise and direct action corresponded better to Angiolini's intent that dance and music alone should suffice to convey the meaning of what happens; toward which purpose Angiolini (who was a musician and at times composed the music for his ballets) even seems to recognize the predominance of music in his program:

> Music is essential to pantomime; it is music that speaks, we only make gestures, similar in this to the actors of tragedy and comedy in antiquity who had others declaim the verses of the work and limited themselves to gesticulation. It would be impossible for us to make ourselves understood without music, and the more appropriate it is, the more it renders us intelligible.[35]

Before this passage, he pays homage to Gluck: "He has grasped perfectly the awesomeness of the action. He has studied how to express the passions that are at play here and the terror that reigns in the catastrophe." He had indeed come across a musician whose inventive vein was none too rich, but who had a lively and adaptable intelligence, who had refined his own musical qualities and his own dramatic intuition over the course of very diverse experiences, and who would soon set about composing, in close collaboration with Calzabigi, *Orfeo ed Euridice* (also performed at the Burgtheater, 5 October 1762, with the collaboration of Angiolini as choreographer). Before establishing himself in Vienna in 1752, Gluck had composed a good number of *opere serie*, for the most part to libretti by Metastasio.[36]

In Vienna, Count Giacomo Durazzo, the principal organizer of court spectacles, had employed him in the most varied activities, above all having him arrange, adapt and at times partially remake or enrich with his own pieces, French *comédies mêlées d'ariettes* and finally having him compose new ones of his own, which enjoyed considerable success (for example, *L'ivrogne corrigé* [The Drunkard Reformed], *Le cadi dupé* [The Duped Judge], and, after the premiere of *Orfeo ed Euridice*, *La rencontre imprévue* [The Unexpected Meeting], which confirmed his new dramatic concept). He therefore had the necessary talents and experience to highlight the most brilliant parts of the ballet and underline the rare humorous impulses; but Angiolini's talents and Zinzendorf's comments show us clearly that the strongest and most enduring impression was that of the Allegro finale, spectral at the beginning in its angular and chromatic design whispered by the basses, later tumultuous in the rapid incursions of the violins and winds, in the livid notes of the brass and in the roar of the entire orchestra for the horrid dance of the furies. At a later performance, Zinzendorf shows that he was also struck by the dark desolation of the penultimate piece, the Larghetto that accompanies the graveyard scene.

The other pieces are also, as Angiolini would have it, "appropriate" in elegant and expert craftsmanship. To particular effect is the serenade with the oboe melody supported by pizzicato violins (no. 2), the duel scene with the briefest tragic pause after which the strings once more take up their thrashing (no. 5) and the scene of fearful trembling, alternating with the vain arrogance of Don Giovanni who fails to reassure his guests. Despite the diversity of subjects, of the means to realize them, and consequently the proportions of the work, one recognizes the tendency toward linearity, the prominence of contrasts, the clarity of outline and—in the highest moments—the intensity of expression that will be characteristic of the operas of Gluck's reform. A different side of the coin shows that Gluck was a good judge of the greater or lesser felicity of his music and had the good ear of a disinterested pragmatist to recognize the capacity of the same music to be "reappropriated" for different situations; he will reuse nos. 18, 21, and 22, transposing them from the banquet in the house of a Spanish nobleman to a classical ballet in Act I of *Iphigénie en Aulide*. He did not dare reuse the music of the dance of the furies, too vivid in the recent memory of the Viennese public, in *Orfeo ed Euridice* of 1762, but he inserted it in his arrangement of the work for Paris in 1774.[37]

4. Don Giovanni in Comic Opera

"At the end of the eighteenth century, Don Giovanni, confused with the literature of libertines, seemed to have exhausted its cycle"; he had to be "liberated from the dark, frozen world and committed to the coarse hands of comedians, who treated him like a puppet whose end no one believed in any longer." Giovanni Macchia's investigation[38] of "Don Giovanni Before Mozart"[39] confirms this observation, showing that even in the musical field the theme flourished for the most part in the provinces or outside Italy, in places that lacked a tradition of regular operatic performances, carried there by the equivalent of rough-handed comedians, impresarios who did not care about subtleties, at the head of more or less itinerant companies. Their activity is difficult to reconstruct because the libretti, valuable sources of information about dates and places of performance, even if they were printed, have a much lower survival rate than those that were systematically collected and preserved where there was a continuity of operatic performance; and those that survive are scattered in libraries of various types and rarely indicated in the largest bibliographies of operatic literature. Of the few that are known it is understandable that they belong almost exclusively to the comic genre, both because the companies that performed them could not afford the luxury of singers of *opera seria*, and because those companies brought opera to places with little exposure to *opera seria*, where audiences were unaccustomed to the artificial conventions of that genre.

They did not, however, renounce profiting from the genre's prestige in order to enlist the unsophisticated public's favor with the pretext of offering them the same pomp in costumes, scenery, and ingenious machines, which the mentality of those days associated with serious theater. It suffices to mention the earliest known eighteenth-century opera on the subject of Don Giovanni,[40] *La pravità castigata* [Trickedness Punished], *dramma per musica* presented in 1734 at the Teatro novissimo della Taverna [!] in Brünn [today Brno] by the new theatrical troupe led by the impresarios Pietro and Angelo Mingotti.[41] Singers who were rather well known in Venice performed *La pravità castigata*, but they were not of the first rank; the most extensive roles were given to Rosa Cardini (Don Giovanni)[42] and the *buffo* Bartolomeo Cajo (Don Giovanni's servant, Malorco). Also assigned to women were the roles of King Manfred of Naples (the action takes place in Naples and its environs) and of his counselor Don Garzia. The most important female roles were given to Teresa Peruzzi "detta Denzia di Venezia" (Donna Isabella) and Cecilia Monti (the fishermaid Rosalba), who also acted during the intermezzi (along with Cajo, who performed the role of the servant) and who was therefore certainly the company's *prima buffa*.[43]

The addition of intermezzi to an opera that already had comic characters is an indication of the assimilation of *opera seria*; aside from this, an address to the "Discreet Reader" (confirming Macchia's diagnosis) does not hesitate to boast in one pen stroke of the exemplary nature of the heavenly punishment that "follows with a duplicated and rare wonder" along with "the rare stylishness of the costumes, the frequent changes of scene, and the measured . . . verse," which are attributes of *opera seria*. Added to this is also "the music of the arias (obtained in an adventurous manner) by an author who often pleases the first monarch of the world"; but whatever musician at the Viennese court might be alluded to here, his adventurous contribution is given a new dimension with the statement: "The music is by Sig. Eustachio Bambini of Pesaro with the exception of a few arias."[44] This clearly indicates what is usually referred to as a "pasticcio"[45] arranged by a musician of whom little is known, except that, having in turn become an impresario, he took his company to Paris in 1752 for the series of performances that led to the *Querelle des Bouffons*.

We can now perhaps identify the contribution of the composer dear to the "first monarch of the world" through a trick with which Mingotti and Bambini abused the dramatic logic and the trust of an unsophisticated audience. In the bilingual libretto there are discrepancies between several of the Italian aria texts and the presumed translations into German. For example, Act I, scene vii, has a German text in which the king of Naples expresses his joy over the alliances concluded by the Commendatore and the prospect of a Christendom united against the Turks; the corresponding Italian text (of a borrowed aria?) describes an innocent little boy attracted by the brilliant colors of an asp and unaware of the dangers it poses. Despite the lack of impresarial scruples, there is an aspect of the libretto of *La pravità* that in a way redeems them: it is possible to speculate that Gluck, who later worked with the Mingotti brothers, might have been acquainted with the final scene in which the imperious defiance of the demons, "Never, never, never!," contrasts with the supplications of the condemned sinner, all of this remarkably similar to a powerful scene in *Orfeo ed Euridice*.

The music of *La pravità* does not survive; it will suffice therefore briefly to summarize the plot, which is a simplified derivative of the plot of Tirso's comedy; however, it does have modifications of the derivations from its Spanish prototype, along with new departures, both probably suggested, at least in part, by the traditions of the commedia dell'arte. Act I begins with the shipwreck of Don Giovanni and Malorco; they are rescued by Rosalba, whom Don Giovanni courts, conquers and immediately abandons. In Act II, Don Giovanni uses subterfuge to introduce himself into Donna Beatrice's rooms, is discovered, but succeeds in laying blame on Duke Ottavio; immediately afterward, he tries to take Donna Isabella violently and kills her father who has run to her aid. Act III witnesses the reciprocal invitations to dinner between Don Giovanni and the statue of the Commendatore and the disappearance of Don Giovanni into a fiery vortex, after which the weddings of Donna Beatrice to Don Garzia and of Donna Isabella to Duke Ottavio take place. New departures with regard to Tirso (but already noted elsewhere) include Don Giovanni's attempt to make Rosalba appear mad, the remonstrances of Malorco to his master, the list of conquests that the same Malorco shows Rosalba, and the final vision of hell, most welcome in an opera that boasts a richness in scenic effects. To Stefan Kunze, this opera appears to be a vestige of an antiquated type of comic opera that predates Zeno's reform.[46] To me, it seems, as I have already noted, that it owes its ambiguous characteristics to the attempt to offer a public relatively unused to operatic theater a spectacle which, without renouncing many comic elements, would also possess the prestige of *opera seria*.

There may have been other such productions; for us, however, there is a gap of more than forty years between *La pravità castigata* of 1734 and *Il convitato di pietra, o sia Il dissoluto*, libretto by Nunziato Porta set to music by Vincenzo Righini and performed in Prague in 1776 and 1777, in Vienna also in 1777, and at Eszterháza (with additions by Haydn) in 1781 and 1782.[47]

Such late dates render even less likely than for *La pravità castigata* Kunze's reference to a *dramma serioridicolo* that originated before Zeno and Metastasio;[47] also in Prague the frequent opera performances were usually given by traveling companies, so that once more the hybrid characteristics of the opera may instead stem from the ambivalence of a company that sought to increase the attractiveness of the comic genre by combining it with the decorum and decoration (staged with the greatest economy possible) of *opera seria* (Kunze seems also unaware of the variety of stances that consistently characterized comic opera). In this sense, one can interpret that alternation from one act to the next of elements derived from Tirso's original filtered through the commedia dell'arte with others drawn from the model of Goldoni, of whom Porta shows himself a fervent admirer and, in his own way, emulator.

The opera again takes up Goldoni's alternative title (*Il dissoluto*) and his generic label (*dramma tragicomico*); but is is difficult to judge from Kunze's summary precisely what elements are derived from this model. Its beginning does not follow Goldoni: it begins with the shipwreck and rescue of Don Giovanni (who has fled Naples after having seduced Donna Isabella) along with Arlecchino his servant; the fishermaid Elisa who rescues him (her name is that of Goldoni's shepherdess) has a fiancé, but this does not stop her from letting Don Giovanni seduce her. A second group of scenes is derived from Acts II and III of Goldoni's version: the minister Don Alfonso announces that the king of Castile wants to reward the services that the Commendatore of Loioa has rendered him by having a monument built to him while he is still alive and giving his daughter, Donna Anna, to Don Ottavio, whom she detests; meanwhile, disquieting news of Don Giovanni's misdeeds arrives at the court. In another traditional sequence, Don Giovanni introduces himself into Donna Anna's house; she resists him, and the Commendatore intervenes and is killed in a duel; Donna Anna cries (or sings) vengeance. In Act II, the order of events is even more disconnected (also because of the difficulty of reducing to three acts elements derived from Goldoni's five): Don Giovanni decides to leave, but in the meantime he orders Arlecchino to have dinner prepared at the inn where he is lodging; Donna Isabella, having arrived from Naples, pleads with the minister to have Don Giovanni punished; Don Giovanni seeks out the Commendatore's tomb; there he is met by Donna Anna and begs mercy of her; then through Arlecchino he invites the statue to dinner. Again at court, Donna Anna obtains from the minister the promise that her father's murderer will be punished. At the inn, Don Giovanni's dinner is served by Arlecchino, the serving girl Corallina (a generic derivation from Goldoni) and the innkeeper Tiburzio; perhaps for the first time in an opera on this subject appear the drinking songs that Don Giovanni and Arlecchino address to the city in which the opera is being performed and to its women (taken from the customs of the commedia dell'arte, they are suited to a traveling company), until the statue's arrival causes general confusion and terror. In Act III, the meal offered in turn by the statue ends with the disappearance of the unrepentant sinner amidst the flames of hell; Arlecchino informs Don Alfonso and Donna Anna of this. In the finale, Don Giovanni is surrounded by furies who enumerate his sins in a chorus. Despite his admiration for the Venetian playwright, Porta did not renounce the traditional elements of the comic servant, the meals with the statue, and the scene in hell, and his awkward derivation is apparent also in the fact that the character Don Ottavio, mentioned in Act I as the husband destined to Donna Anna, who hates him, is completely abandoned and never appears in the opera.

The Bolognese Vincenzo Righini (1756–1812) was Mozart's exact contemporary and may have studied with Padre Martini, like him; he was barely twenty years old and had come to Prague engaged as tenor in the company of the impresario Giuseppe Bustelli. We do not know how he instead came to be employed in writing the music of *Il convitato*; but his debut as a composer was certainly a success, to the extent that in 1778 he wrote two more operas for Prague that were inspired by Goldoni, *La vedova scaltra* [The Resorceful Widow] (also performed that same spring in Brescia) and *La bottega del caffè* [The Coffee House]. In 1780, he was called to Vienna as the singing master of the Archduchess Elisabeth and also was given managerial responsibility as director of the Italian comic opera. There he came to know Mozart (who provided an assessment of him that was only partially favorable) and Da Ponte, who wrote for him the libretto of *Demogorgone o Il filosofo confuso* (it was produced in Vienna in 1786 with success, but described by Da Ponte as infelicitous). Thus, his *Convitato* could be, in a certain sense, a direct antecedent to Mozart's masterpiece; having to judge this through indirect evidence,[49] I can only highlight the importance that was given the finales of the three acts, especially that of Act II.[50] This may also have been a reflection of the extension and variety that Goldoni gave to comic finales.

An echo of the success of *Il convitato* by Porta and Righini was the *Don Juan albo Ukarany libertyn* (*Don Giovanni ossia Il dissoluto*) presented in Polish in Warsaw in 1783 with music by Joachim Albertini (1748–1812) to a libretto that was in part a translation, in part a reworking, of that by Nunziato Porta.[51] Later it was restaged in Italian at the Teatro della Pergola in Florence (1792), and the only surviving score stems from that production, in which, in comparison to Righini's original, one notes the tendency to accentuate the tragic moments of the action and to make more ample use of the chorus.[52] In certain passages of the Florentine text, which present verbal parallels to the development of corresponding situations in the libretto written by Da Ponte in 1787 for Mozart, it is difficult to say if it is matter of anticipations or echoes. At issue here are above all phrases assigned Ercolino (i.e., Righini's Arlecchino, who here has been changed to an Italian character, who does not speak in dialect): "Egli è lo sposatore universale, / sian giovani, sian vecchie, belle, o brutte, / è un uomo di buon cor, le sposa tutte" ["He is the universal husband; / Be they young, old, fair, or ugly, / He is a man of good heart / Who marries them all"]; and, in the invitation to the statue: "Signor commendatore stimatissimo, / Padrone colendissimo, / il mio Padron v'invita" ["Most esteemed commander, / Most respected master, / My master invites you"].

In Italy, the first operatic *Convitato di pietra* of the eighteenth-century that we know of is the one (to an anonymous libretto) that was performed with music by Giuseppe Calegari at the Teatro San Cassiano in Venice in 1777, a year after the first production in Prague of Righini's opera. Calegari, born in Padua (ca. 1750),[53] was the older of two brothers both of whom were opera composers and impresarios of opera companies. The old Teatro San Cassiano had recently been renovated, but it does not seem as to have attracted a large audience; none other than Giacomo Casanova had informed the authorities a year earlier that male and female prostitutes infested the two upper ranks of boxes.[54] Calegari revealed his impresarial instincts in assigning the role of Donna Anna, Donna Isabella, and the fishermaid Rosalba to a single singer, the *prima buffa* Geltrude Flavis. Don Giovanni, listed in the libretto as *primo buffo di mezzo carattere*, was sung by the baritone Domenico Madrigali; his servant Pallarino was labelled a *buffo caricato*.[55]

Working in the Venetian theatrical environment, which was still an important center for the recruitment of singers, Calegari may have been aware of Righini;[56] but his *dramma giocoso per musica* in two acts (a division that precisely in this decade became the favored one for comic operas) develops far more rapidly and directly, without the too frequent changes of scene and the tortuous returns of the Prague libretto. Don Giovanni's adventures with Donna Isabella, the fishermaid Rosalba, and Donna Anna are faithfully derived from Tirso's comedy (including the names of the two ladies), but they are simplified to the point that they are all concluded in Act I. The opera opens with the dispute between Don Giovanni and Donna Isabella, similar to the one between Don Giovanni and Donna Anna at the beginning of Mozart's opera; but as in Tirso's *Burlador*, a duel does not ensue, that being left to the final episode in the finale of Act I; and aside from this, the opening scene is followed (rather than preceded) by the laments of the servant who is waiting for his master and curses his destiny. New to the musical stage (but deriving from the commedia dell'arte) is a jesting dialogue between Don Giovanni and his servant (named Passarino) who do not recognize each other in the dark and come to blows until the misunderstanding is clarified. At the end of the act, Don Giovanni introduces himself into Donna Anna's house pretending to be Don Ottavio and is inside while the actual Don Ottavio is outside serenading her; the intervention and murder of the Commendatore close the act. After this, the prosecution of Don Giovanni's crimes unfolds, first at court and later in the graveyard scene; the dinner offered by Don Giovanni (with a drinking song in praise of Venice) and the dinner offered by the statue follow. After Don Giovanni disappears, the finale is full of joy and exaltation. Typical of the realistic bent that comic opera had taken on by this time is the absence among the singers of both castrati and women assuming male roles.

Chapter Three: The Immediate Antecedents of Mozart

1. Giambattista Lorenzi and Giacomo Tritto

In Naples, comic theater, whether spoken or musical, often used dialect, or at least a mixture of standard Italian with the local dialect; conforming to this usage are two new eighteenth-century incarnations of the myth of Don Giovanni, a *Nuovo convitato di pietra* by the artisan-playwright Francesco Cerlone (a prose comedy Cerlone may have repudiated, which has only recently been redis-covered)[1] and a one-act farce bearing the same title but without any pretension to the novelty implied in that title, a farce that the Arcadian Giambattista Lorenzi offered to the composer Giacomo Tritto. The work I have labelled as a "farce" is presented in the libretto of *Li due gemelli, ed Il convitato di pietra* [The Two Twins and The Stone Guest] as the second of two "*commedie in un atto per musica* . . . to be performed in the new Teatro dei Fiorentini for this year's carnival of 1783" because the score defines it as farce and because it manifests the tendency to accentuate the most

69

highly caricatured aspects of the plot to the point of using an idiomatic dialect. The introduction of Pulcinella, a mask who speaks in dialect, as Don Giovanni's servant—among the pushiest, most talkative servants—brings it close to the most clownish genres of the commedia dell'arte and distinguishes it from other more finely crafted works by Lorenzi, such as L'idolo cinese [The Chinese Idol] (1767), Il Socrate immaginario [The Man Who Believed He Was Socrates] (1775), La scuffiara [The Milliner] (1784), and Nina pazza per amore [Nina, the love-crazed maid] (1789), all set to music by Paisiello.[2] Aside from his libretti for Paisiello, to whom he was particularly attached, Lorenzi (1721–1807), a very well-known figure in Neapolitan theatrical circles and a connoisseur of not only Italian, but also French contemporary literature, had written comic libretti for several other well-known Neapolitan composers, such as Porpora, Astaritta, and Piccinni.[3] He must have taken in his stride his collaboration with Tritto (1733–1824), who, though already fifty years old, had only recently experienced one of the most prosperous seasons in his career as an opera composer of some success, a career for the most part restricted to theaters in Naples and Rome.[4] Or perhaps it seemed to him that the inevitable punishment of the reprobate inherent in the fable was sufficient to reaffirm the aim he had formulated some years earlier in L'infedeltà fedele [Infidelity Proven Faithful] (produced in 1779 with music by Cimarosa): "to season fables moderately" and "to place proper emphasis on the tragedy I have introduced here, which has not previously been introduced into musical farces."[5]

The cast list in the libretto opens with the name of "Lesbina the peasant girl promised to Pulcinella," sung by a prima buffa toscana, Celeste Coltellini, who in that decade had enjoyed great success not only in Naples but also in Vienna;[6] and the role of Don Giovanni Tenorio, the third from last on the list, is almost crushed by the intrusions of Pulcinella and by the frequent appearances onstage of Lesbina with her father Bastiano, both of whom, flattered by Don Giovanni's fleeting advances, assume ridiculous airs of nobility and exchange the titles "Count" and "Countess." Along with the purely verbal conquest of Lesbina and the attempted but unconsummated conquest of Donna Anna di Ulloa (which leads to the murder of her father), the protagonist's fame as a seducer is confirmed only by the brief appearances of the Marquesa Isabella "from Pellegrina, betrayed by Don Giovanni" and by the comments that Don Giovanni himself makes in the least opportune moments on the physical attributes of Donna Anna's servant, Chiarella (who also sings in Neapolitan dialect, even though the action takes place in Seville), and the innkeeper's wife whom he has barely glimpsed. The entire story is further compressed through the reduction into one act to only three of the essential moments:[7] (1) the substitution of Don Giovanni for Don Ottavio in his secret meeting with Donna Anna, followed by the duel and the murder of the Commendatore; (2) the accusations directed at Don Giovanni by Isabella and Anna, which lead to the condemnation of the guilty party by one of the king's ministers and to his taking refuge in a "church with the equestrian statue of the Commendatore"; and (3) at the end, the death of the sinner (and the sight of him in hell), which renders the prosecutors' fury vain. But even thus reduced it still meanders tortuously, and even though in one act is still none too brief; there is, furthermore, in the above-mentioned autograph score preserved in Naples a sign of a subdivision into two parts, each of which closes with the noise of an ensemble.[8]

The score opens with an overture, a single-movement Allegro in which all the forces that will provide the instrumental resources of the opera participate: two oboes, two horns, and strings.[9] Beginning with the first theme (which will not be repeated even in the closing section), vigorous, rhythmically pronounced accents prevail, barely softened by the more cantabile theme that provides the modulatory section. The piece flows pleasantly; we are, however, far from a sonata-form movement, neither does it announce any of the musical themes that will appear in the course of the opera. As a recent historian of Neapolitan opera has observed: "There was no point in trying, within the overture, to enchant an audience that would not listen anyway";[10] that the overture was only a signal, a call to attention, is confirmed by the contrast between its brilliant conclusion in G major and the whispered nocturnal Andante in E-flat major that follows with the rising of the curtain. We are *in medias res*: it is nighttime, and a tenor Don Giovanni wearing the hat and cape of Don Ottavio (who will never appear onstage) has come to take the latter's place beneath Donna Anna's windows for a serenade that is the agreed signal for a secret meeting.

In addition to its nocturnal atmosphere, this beginning also shares with Mozart's opera its title "introduction" in the score, which in the operatic jargon of the day designated (as did the term "finale") a rapid progression of closely linked scenes. Also in this instance, although without the same continuity and intensity, events will lead rapidly to a dramatic climax; but for the moment the low murmuring of the violins accompanies a dialogue in which Pulcinella inserts the comedy of his jests and jargon; and even when Don Giovanni's song blossoms persuasively for the serenade, he will be counterpointed with the caricatured imitation of Pulcinella:

Giovanni
Chiudi presto la lanterna,
ch'io non voglio esser veduto.
Tu ci senti?

Pulcinella
    Aggio sentuto
ma a lo manco na lucerna
fammer prima procurà.

Giovanni
Close the lantern;
I do not want to be seen.
Do you hear me?

Pulcinella
    I heard you,
But I don't even have a lamp.
I first have to get one.

Giovanni
Perché mai?

Pulcinella
      Oh chesta è bella!
Stuto chesta, e addummo chella,
pe bederce a cammenà.

Giovanni
Chiudi, bestia.

Pulcinella
      È chiusa già.

Giovanni
Pulcinella?

Pulcinella
      Che bolite?

Giovanni
Sono pronti i Suonatori?
  (Pulcinella cala la testa)
Pulcinella?

Pulcinella
      Gno? decite.

Giovanni
Sono pronti? Presto dì . . .
  (come sopra)

Pulcinella
E non bide, ca da n'ora
co la capo dico sì.

Giovanni
Why?

Pulcinella
      Oh, that's rich!
I'll put this one out, and light that one,
So that we can see where we're going.

Giovanni
Close it, fool.

Pulcinella
      It's already closed.

Giovanni
Pulcinella?

Pulcinella
      What is it?

Giovanni
Are the players ready?
  (Pulcinella nods his head.)
Pulcinella?

Pulcinella
      Sir, you were saying?

Giovanni
Are they ready? Quickly, tell me.
  (as above)

Pulcinella
Eh, don't you see for an hour already
I've been nodding with my head?

Giovanni
Ma che sciocco! Via poltrone:
fa suonare, che si fa?

Pulcinella
Priesto a buie, ca lo Patrone
ave voglia d'arraglià.

(Si suona, e Don Giovanni canta)

Giovanni
Ombre amiche, amici orrori,
fide scorte degli amanti,
qui per voi tra poch'istanti
il mio Sol vagheggerò.

Pulcinella
(Scope amiche, amiche mazze,
fide scorte de i birbanti,
il Padron fra poch'istanti
zoppicar per voi vedrò).

Giovanni   Giovanni
Che mai dici, temerario?
che mai brontoli, si sa?

Pulcinella   Pulcinella
Ca stanotte il Calannario
mette secce in quantità.

Giovanni
What a fool you are! Go on, sluggard:
Have them play. What are you doing?

Pulcinella
Quick! The master
Wants to bray in the dark.

(They play, and Don Giovanni sings)

Giovanni
Friendly shadows, friendly horrors,
Faithful escorts to lovers.
Here in a few moments
I will woo my sun because of you.

Pulcinella
(Friendly brooms, friendly cudgels,
Faithful escorts of rogues,
In a few moments, my master
Will hobble because of you.)

What are you saying, rash man?
What are you mumbling?

That tonight your calendar
Is very full.

The orchestra's accompaniment continues during the whispers Don Giovanni exchanges with Chiarella; she believes she recognizes Don Ottavio and promises to come down to let him in; while waiting, Don Giovanni has a new lyric piece, once more aped by Pulcinella. The serenade and this new melodious rush (see

Example 8), although they are not solos, are Don Giovanni's best moments of song, the only ones in which he is granted full melodic effusion and not restricted, as in the rest of the opera, to recitatives and ensembles.

The propulsive thrust of the introduction is attenuated now in a series of recitatives: before Chiarella descends to let Don Giovanni into the house, there is still time for Pulcinella to reproach him for his offenses, which, however, are restricted to the dangers he encountered in Naples with "Donna Sabella" and in Mallorca with "Tisbea the fishermaid"; and also in recitative are the laments of the servant left alone to wait during the night, here with the unusual variant of Pulcinella's prospective wedding:

Pulcinella
Aibò, non è chiù cosa de tenerlo
a patrone co mmico. Craje matina
voglio agghiustà li cunte:
si m'ha da dà, mme paga; e si ha
   d'avere,
non 'nce ne parlo affatto, e ne lo
   manno.
Io già stongo appuntato
de mme sposà Lesbina,
ch'è meza meza pajesana mia:
essa ha no buono territorio, e io
pozzo a sciore campà 'ncopp' a
   lo mio.
Agua . . . *(sbadiglia)* lo suonno già
   mme va zucanno . . .
Non c'è che dì: sò cani li patrune
con nuje sette panelle:
nce levano la pelle
pe dì rana lo mese,
ma l'agghiustammo nuje 'ncopp'a
   le spese.

Pulcinella
Oh no, there's nothing more to tie me
To my master. Tomorrow morning,
I want to settle my account.
If he owes me, he should pay me; if
   I owe him,
We won't speak of it. I'll just go.

I have already decided
To marry Lesbina,
Who's almost one of my own people.
She has some good land, and I
Can grow some wheat to live off
   mine.
Water . . . *(He yawns.)* Sleep is
   overtaking me . . .
There's no denying, masters are dogs.
For seven loaves of bread
They scold us mercilessly
For ten cents a month.
But we will settle up about the
   expenses.

One suddenly hears the voice of the Commendatore inside; fleeing him, Don Giovanni jumps from the balcony and gets into a comic scuffle with Pulcinella who, before recognizing him in the dark holds his head and drags him along the ground while Don Giovanni holds his sword up high in order not to be hit (all this is in recitative).[11] Soon afterward, the introduction ends with the eruption onto the stage of the Commendatore, the brief duel, the final death stroke, all still in recitative, now strongly dramatic and accompanied by strings (Example 9). An aria follows, at first restrained, then dramatically excited, in which Donna Anna expresses her sorrow and her remorse.

The sets must have been modest at the Teatro dei Fiorentini and the set changes rapid, to judge from frequent indications in the score like the one that precedes scene v ("follows immediately").[12] We are now in "a countryside with rustic abodes" with Lesbina, Pulcinella, and Bastiano who rejoice singing and dancing "to the sound of a bagpipe, drum, and other folk instruments"; their tarantella is no less Neapolitan than Pulcinella's dialect, which Lesbina, who has come to Seville from Naples where she was born, gradually adopts. In the recitative that follows, Lesbina plays the shy and modest girl with Pulcinella; but when Don Giovanni arrives in the meantime to the surprise and disappointment of Pulcinella, it takes but a fleeting compliment from him for her to remark to herself, "I like him more that I do Pulcinella." Under his breath, Don Giovanni gets right to the point:

Giovanni	*Giovanni*
(Quanto mi piaci! e se tu vuoi ti sposo)	(I love you so much! And if you want, I'll marry you.)

Lesbina	*Lesbina*
(E se voi mi sposate,	(And if you marry me,
mi chiameranno poi Donna Lesbina?)	Will they call me "Lady Lesbina"?)
Giovanni	*Giovanni*
(Anzi il titolo avrai di Contessina)	(Better still, you will have the title
	of countess.)

However, he tells Lesbina to continue to pretend to love Pulcinella, and he himself embraces Pulcinella to appease him, but, before leaving, furtively gives her his hand behind Pulcinella's back. Pulcinella's remonstrances lead to a duet in the course of which she gradually calms him down; but this does not prevent her from leaving to meet Don Giovanni while Pulcinella is still singing. Pulcinella remains alone face to face with Bastiano who demands his daughter back from him; Pulcinella declares he no longer wants to marry her and leaves Bastiano alone to boast about the virtues of all the women of his family in an aria that is accompanied by strings alone, as befits a secondary character.

A new change of scene (scene ix) leads us to the house of the Marquis Dorasquez, the king's minister, who learns from Donna Isabella how Don Giovanni seduced and abandoned her in Naples; Donna Anna also arrives, with her servant Chiarella, to demand justice for the man who killed the Commendatore. Still in recitative, Don Giovanni, the last to arrive, can only make vague protests against the marquis' questions and the protests of the ladies who together assail him; and the marquis can only order the arrest and participate with the others in the quintet that concludes the first part of the opera, which returns to the opening key of the act, E-flat major. In this quintet, operatic tradition allows each character to spend most of the time expressing to him- or herself reflections unheard by the others (scene x; see Example 10):

Giovanni
Cedo; il comando impresso
nel cor mi resterà.
   (resta pensieroso)

Marchese
(Lo vedo assai perplesso:
segno di reità.)

Isabella
(In quel suo volto espresso
veggo il rimorso già.)

Anna
(Il suo delitto istesso
già lo tormenterà.)

Chiarella
(Va trova; a lo prociesso
chillo mò penzarrà.)

Marchese
(Non parla.)

Isabella
     (Non ha fiato.)

Anna
(È un tronco.)

Chiarella
     (S'è agghiajato.)

Isabella e Anna
(La colpa atroce e nera
lo deve lacerar.)

Giovanni
I yield. The command will remain
Etched on my heart.
   (He remains thoughtful.)

Marquis Dorasquez
(I see he is very perplexed:
A sign of his guilt.)

Isabella
(I see from his facial expression
He is already full of remorse.)

Anna
(His very crime
Will itself torment him.)

Chiarella
(What do you know; the trial,
That's what he's thinking of.)

Marquis Dorasquez
(He does not speak.)

Isabella
     (He's out of breath.)

Anna
(He's stone silent.)

Chiarella
     (He has turned to ice.)

Isabella and Anna
(The black, atrocious crime
Must be harrowing him.)

Giovanni
(No: quella Cameriera
   [guardando Chiarella]
non è da disprezzar.)

Giovanni
(No, that chambermaid
   [looking at Chiarella]
Is not to be disdained.)

A quattro
Comprendi il fallo enorme?
Tremi all'error commesso?

All Four
Do you see the enormity of the crime?
Do you tremble for the error you
   have committed?

Ma la clemenza dorme,
ma è morta la pietà.

But clemency sleeps,
And pity is dead.

Giovanni
Trema chi è delinquente:
chi dalla colpa è oppresso;
ma un'anima innocente
tremar giammai non sa.

Giovanni
The guilty tremble,
Those oppressed with guilt;
An innocent soul
Never trembles.

This situation already anticipates the close of the Act I finale of Mozart's opera ("Trema, trema, o scellerato"); but there it will involve seven voices plus chorus, while here, with neither chorus nor basses the sonority is necessarily more modest (Pulcinella and Bastiano, the two basses in the cast, are absent, and present instead are the two tenors, Don Giovanni and the marquis). The usual repetitions of words (not indicated in the libretto) permit the last eight lines to be sung repeatedly by all present.

The second part takes us back to the city and Pulcinella, who again reflects on his relationship with Don Giovanni (scene xi); he is interrupted (scene xii) by "Lesbina dressed *in adriè*, Bastiano in a rich nobleman's tunic and carrying a parasol, and some peasants dressed as servants"—an exhibition of pompous lordly pretensions in which they address each other in turn as "Father, count" and "Daughter, countess." Pulcinella's ironic grins (scene xiii) are followed by the arrival of Don Giovanni who sends them to the devil; he has escaped arrest (later we will discover how), and hastily orders Pulcinella to follow him "to the nearby church to save himself." After so much dialogue, nothing remains for the poor abandoned countess but to sing an aria that in its opening melodic figure (Example 11) and in its alternation of an Allegretto full of pathos with faster sections is reminiscent of the aria "A Serpina penserete," which almost a half century earlier Pergolesi had written for his servant mistress—an indication of how deeply Tritto was immersed in the tradition of Neapolitan comic opera. It is the second piece designed to show Coltellini's interpretive gifts and the variety of her expressive stances:

Dov'è più la Contessina?	Where now is the countess?
Dove andò la nobiltà?	Where has the nobility gone?
Della povera Lesbina	For poor Lesbina,
chi mai sente, oh Dio! pietà?	Who, oh God, will feel pity?
Ma qui ferma, disleale:	But hold, false one.
non fuggirmi, traditore:	Traitor, do not flee.
o trafiggi questo core,	Either stab this heart
o ritornami ad amar.	Or love me once more.
Ma pentito il caro bene	But repentant my dear treasure
già mi viene a consolar.	Already comes to console me.
Già si fanno le mie nozze:	My wedding is set already:
che fracasso d'istromenti:	What noise of instruments:
che rumore di carrozze . . .	What noise of carriages . . .
Ma lo sposo mio dov'è?	But where is the groom?
Uh! che pianto! . . . che singhiozzo!	Ah! what tears! . . . what sobs?
Io mi affoco . . . io mi strozzo . . .	I am raging . . . I am choking . . .
Non vi son più giuramenti:	There are no more oaths.
no, non v'è più fedeltà.	No, there is no more fidelity.

Don Giovanni and Pulcinella having already exited, now the count and countess also leave the stage free for the marquis, who announces that an equestrian statue of the Commendatore, which had already been sculpted before he died, has been erected in the church. Donna Anna once more pleads for vengeance, and Donna Isabella arrives to announce that Don Giovanni has fled the arresting officers by once more jumping from the balcony. Isabella now remains alone onstage (scene xv) because it is now her turn to sing an aria (preceded by regrets expressed in a brief recitative), an aria in which she admonishes all women to be cautious and not to believe in a lover's tears.

Scene xvi carries us to the door of the "Temple with the equestrian Statue of the Commendatore," miraculously erected in such a short time. Don Giovanni sees it and interrupts Pulcinella's usual jests to read the inscription: "On him who dragged me to an evil death / I here await my vengeance from heaven." His defiance of the statue and his consequent mocking invitation to dinner lead the way to a very traditional conclusion of the story. The statue's response makes Pulcinella forget his own appetite and induces him to flee, having, however, first expressed the terror he feels in an aria in which the orchestra plays with sharp contrasts between soft passages and forceful accents. Don Giovanni repeats the invitation and he himself goes to the "atrium of the Temple" with a change of scene that occurs before the audience's eyes. Everything that occurs from this point onward constitutes scene xvii, labelled "Finale" in the score, even though there will be three (or perhaps four) changes of scene; and the entire finale, including its brief passages of recitative, will be continuously accompanied by the orchestra, with the addition, perhaps spurious, of two clarinets.[13]

The beginning of the finale restores the key of E-flat major with which the first part closed and which will return once more at the end of the opera. The arrival of a table well prepared with macaroni momentarily allays Pulcinella's fears (from the dialogue we learn that before going to the church Don Giovanni had ordered it from the innkeeper whose wife he had eyed); they hear knocking (produced by the orchestra), and Pulcinella exits and returns fearfully to hide under the table, while Don Giovanni goes to meet the statue. In the exchange that follows, a seemingly familiar phrase recurs ("I cibi miei non son terreni. Io vado" ["My food is not of this earth. I go"] and "L'oscurità non m'impedisce il volo." ["Darkness does not prevent my flight"]), after which the statue, having in turn extended an invitation to Don Giovanni and Pulcinella to dine with him, actually fulfills the stage marvel of flying away (a stage direction in the libretto and Pulcinella's comments attest to this). Another scene change carries us back to the house of the marquis, besieged by Lesbina and Bastiano who demand their respective husband and son-in-law; but Don Giovanni's condemnation, which emanates from the king (which king is unclear) and is announced in the presence of the other three woman also, is inexorable: Don Giovanni must first marry Donna Isabella and then he will be judged. All this forms an animated concerted ensemble, after which the scene changes back to the temple "with a table covered as if in mourning, with black candelabras and candles, and strewn with serpents, frogs, and other poisonous animals"; E-flat major definitively reestablishes itself after having been temporarily abandoned in a sudden digression (another opportunity for Coltellini to grab the spotlight). It is easy to imagine the reactions of Pulcinella, but Don Giovanni is unmoved; at the Commendatore's request, he gives him his hand and even though seized with pain ("Ah what fire . . . Ah what pain! / I feel myself burning up") he remains undaunted ("I do not repent; I am the same man, / Neither does heaven cause me to fear"). He sinks, "the statue flies away, and Pulcinella falls to the ground in fear," just a moment before all the others, along with the guards who were to arrest Don Giovanni, burst onto the stage. After the usual brief narration of the servant, a new wonder of stagecraft occurs: the appearance of hell with the "ghost representing the damned soul of Don Giovanni," who also participates in the concerted ensemble that closes the finale, this time sung by eight voices, though not in eight real parts:

Anima [Larva]
Dove sono? ahi dove caddi?
Son dannato! oimè, che pene!
per un breve, e falso bene
in eterno ho da penar!

Soul [Ghost]
Where am I? Ah, where have I fallen?
I am damned! Alas, what torments!
For a brief, false good
To suffer eternally!

Tutti
Che terrore! che spavento!
che funesta orribil scena!
Per l'orrore in sen mi sento
ogni fibra palpitar.

All
What terror! What fear!
What a woeful, horrible sight!
Horrified I feel
Every fiber in my breast tremble.

Larva
Ahi che sono, me infelice!
da' miei falli atroci, e immondi
negli abbissi più profondi
strascinato a lagrimar.

Ghost
Ah, wretch that I am!
Because of my foul, atrocious errors,
Dragged into the deepest abysses
To weep.

Tutti
Ah che il cor mi trema in petto!

Ahi qual giel mi cadde sopra!
Ecco il fin di chi mal opra:
ecco il Cielo che sa far.

All
Ah, how my heart trembles in my breast!
Ah, how I turn to ice!
This is the end of the evildoer.
This is what heaven can do.

For once, even Pulcinella abandons dialect.

For all its ingenious compression of so much action into one act, this opera is full of imbalances, beginning with the one between the librettist and composer, the latter sacrificed to the exhibitionism of the former, which in great part coincides with the exhibitionism of Pulcinella, expressed for the most part in recitative. To this is added the necessity (once more an impresarial motive) of placing the diva of the moment in the foreground, who has to herself two arias and a duet, while the protagonist has not one opportunity to have the attention all to himself. And this imbalance is also attributable to the imbalance between the two authors. Far from applying the saying "First the music, then the words," we have here an exuberant Lorenzi, even if not at his best as a writer of comedies; to whom Tritto, whose personality and breeding lacked all aggressiveness (which is confirmed by his late entry into the field of opera), could not pose countervailing musical needs. He therefore closely followed the road his librettist had mapped out and did so competently and attentively, with fluent music that always finds the right tone to underline what happens onstage, that has within limits the continuity and animation necessary to bring the work to life, but that lacks the gestures and expressions that would make an enduring impression. One appreciates the rhythmic energy of the music and the overall sense of tonal cohesiveness; but the melodic invention is short-winded and drawn out through repetition, the harmonies are correct but lacking variety, and even his contrapuntal experience, which might have found an outlet in the numerous ensembles, was perhaps inhibited by his practical responsibility not to tax the singers overmuch. The *Don Giovanni* that results from this conforms to the Neapolitan tastes of Lorenzi and Coltellini and is sustained by the workmanlike competence of Tritto.

Tritto's score must have been used for other productions in Naples; this is documented above all by the variants entered into the so-called autograph.[14] Lorenzi's text was more widely circulated, since, deprived of its Neapolitan Pulcinella, it traveled the peninsula accompanied by the music of Vincenzo Fabrizi and often preceded by the first act of *Il capriccio drammatico* [The Dramatic Caprice] (of which I will say more below) or *L'impresario in angustie* [The Impresario in Distress] by Giuseppe Maria Diodati with music by Cimarosa.[15] Neapolitan or Roman and presumably a student of Tritto, Fabrizi (1764–1812?)[16] was certainly more enterprising than his presumed teacher if, barely nineteen years old, he had already produced *I tre gobbi rivali*, an "intermezzo for four voices to be sung by the company of the Comici Lombardi at the Teatro dei Fiorentini for the carnival of 1783" (a reworking of Diodati's setting of Goldoni's *La favola de' tre gobbi*). Fabrizi must have attended Lorenzi's *Convitato* and presented it with his own music (and with the Neapolitan Pulcinella replaced by a certain Ficcanaso) in various Italian cities after its first production at the Teatro Valle in Rome in autumn 1787, his work also anticipating Mozart's by only a short while.[17]

2. Giovanni Bertati and Giuseppe Gazzaniga

A few months before Mozart, in the carnival of 1787, two other opera composers drew upon the story of the punished rake to entertain the Venetians. About the first of these (not necessarily the first to be staged), *Il nuovo convitato di pietra*, to an anonymous libretto set to music by Francesco Gardi, I will speak only briefly. The libretto defines itself as a "*dramma tragicomico* to be presented at the noble Teatro San Samuele"; but it has very little of the tragic about it, and the libretto of the single restaging reduces its novelty, tragedy, and importance to the title *Il convitato di pietra*, "*dramma giocoso da rappresentarsi in musica* by a company of dilettantes in the private Teatro de' due Muri in the summer of 1791."[18] It would merit the label of "farce" with its two comic servants (Zuccasecca and Masone) instead of one, and four women (Donna Anna, Donna Isabella, the fishermaid Tisbea, and the innkeeper Betta), each of whom was seduced by Don Giovanni antecedent to the stage action, and each of whom is pursuing him to make him marry her; they pick on each other and meanwhile accept the company and advances of the servants. It is unlikely that the unknown librettist and the little-known composer were familiar to Mozart and Da Ponte.[19]

The boast of novelty in the title hides the competition with the Teatro San Moisè which had announced a *Don Giovanni o sia Il convitato di pietra* that had its premiere on 5 February as the second act of *Il capriccio drammatico*, "*rappresentazione per musica* by Giovanni Bertati."[20] The music was by a composer who was already well known, though not mentioned in the libretto, Giuseppe Gazzaniga. Act I, which prepares it, returns to the theme of opera satirizing itself, in this instance a traveling operatic troupe "in a German city," whose lack of success induces the impresario Policastro (the theme of impresarial initiatives returns) to suggest restaging "the *commedia in musica* / reduced to one act / that was performed in Provence." The *prima buffa a vicenda*, Ninetta, protests:

Ninetta	*Ninetta*
Piano. Questa Commedia è il *Don Giovanni?*	Just a minute. This comedy is *Don Giovanni?*
Policastro	*Policastro*
Appunto. È il Convitato di Pietra.	Precisely. It's *The Stone Guest.*
Ninetta	*Ninetta*
Uhm!	Uh!

Policastro 　　　　Uhm! Che?	*Policastro* 　　　　Uh! What?
Ninetta 　　　　　Potrebbe darsi che qui in Germania . . . Ma . . .	*Ninetta* 　　　Perhaps Here in Germany . . . But . . .
Policastro 　　　　　Temete forse del suo incontro?	*Policastro* 　　　　Are you perhaps afraid It will be poorly received?
Ninetta 　　　Moltissimo. L'azione è inverosimile; il Libretto è fuori delle regole; la Musica non so che cosa sia; ed infatti preveggio che con questa s'andrà di male 　in peggio.	*Ninetta* 　　　Indeed. The story is improbable. The libretto Doesn't follow the rules. The music cannot be described. And I foresee That with this work things will go 　from bad to worse.

Cavalier Tempesta, patron of one of the divas, also protests,[21] but Policastro easily wins out over the two of them in the argument:

Policastro Signor sì, ve l'accordo. Ma la nostra Commedia ridotta com'ell'è, fra la Spagnuola di Tirso de Molina, tra quella di Molière e quella delli nostri Commedianti, qualunque sia, non fu veduta avanti.	*Policastro* Yes, sir. I am in agreement. But our comedy, Distilled as it is from the Spanish Of Tirso de Molina, Molière's work, And that of our Italian actors, Whatever it is, has not been seen 　before.
Cavaliere E poi d'un Atto solo.	*Cavalier* And furthermore it's in one act.

Policastro	Policastro
Per la musica basta.	Musically it's more than enough.
Certo che ancora in questa	To be sure, there are
vi sono mille, e mille inconvenienti;	Thousands of drawbacks;
ma gl'animi gentili	But these gentle souls,
se qualcosa di buono	If they find some good
trovano nella Musica,	In the music,
nelle decorazioni, e nei soggetti,	In the stage sets, in the actors,
compatire sapran gli altri difetti.	Will excuse the other defects.

The success of *Don Giovanni* reduced to a "comedy within a comedy" is ratified by the restagings that it enjoyed in the following years in Varese (autumn 1787), Bologna and Cittadella (spring 1788), Treviso (summer 1788), Padua and Cremona (autumn 1788), Forlì and Corfù (1789). A production in Pavia (1793) with *L'impresario in rovina* as Act I and *Il convitato di pietra* as Act II belongs instead to a parallel series in which Gazzaniga's *Don Giovanni* is preceded by Cimarosa's *L'impresario in angustie* (performed among other places in Turin, Milan, and Ferrara in 1789). In a third combination, *L'impresario in angustie* precedes Lorenzi's *Convitato*, for the most part with music by Vincenzo Fabrizi, but often also with the interpolation of scenes from Bertati's libretto, which presumably were performed with Gazzaniga's music.[22]

The Trevisan Giovanni Bertati (1735-1815) had since 1763 been a prolific author especially of comic libretti, often for the Teatro San Moisè, and set to music for that theater, or restaged for others, by some of the most famous musicians of his time, including Galuppi, Gazzaniga, Anfossi, Astaritta and, later, Cimarosa (for whom Bertati also wrote the libretto of *Il matrimonio segreto*). Already known in Vienna from several visits there since 1770, in 1791 he succeeded Da Ponte as librettist for the imperial theaters in which Italian operas were performed; he remained there through 1794. Giuseppe Gazzaniga (1743–1818), a Veronese who studied with Porpora and Piccinni in Naples, had his debut as an opera composer in 1768; he later had numerous operas performed in Venice as well as in other Italian cities and also enjoyed moderate success even outside Italy. In Vienna, his *Il finto cieco* [The Pretended Blind Man] to a libretto by Da Ponte had been performed in 1786.[23] Bertati and Gazzaniga had often worked together since 1771; during the 1786–1787 season they were occupied through 26 December in the preparation for *L'amor costante*, the new opera that opened the season at the Teatro San Moisè. The choice of *Il capriccio drammatico* as the second opera was probably an expedient to save time; its second act is none other than a lightly modified version of Act I of *La novità* [The Novelty], also by Bertati, which had been performed in 1775 in the same theater with as its second act *L'italiano a Parigi* [The Italian in Paris], both to the music of Felice Alessandri.[24] By adopting the text and music, the librettist and musician reduced their task to the composition of only one new act.

To this circumstance is owed the concision that the diffuse story of Don Giovanni acquires in the new single act, still derived from several elements in Molière along with traditional ones. The role of Elvira derives from Molière; and since Elvira substitutes for Tirso's Isabella, the opening altercation between Isabella and Don Giovanni (still present in Calegari's opera of 1777) was transferred to Donna Anna and Don Giovanni and is followed by the murder of the Commendatore (a more rapid and effective solution than the analogous one of Lorenzi and Tritto, because it eliminates the opening serenade). From Molière derives the character Maturina (along with her name) and her rustic fiancé Biagio (named Pierrot in Molière). Stefan Kunze rightly observes that the number and quality of singers available must have influenced the outline of the plot; there were eight voices in all, among which three were women's.[25] It would have been logical to assign to the three women the parts of Donna Anna, Donna Elvira, and Maturina, but the limit-ed capacity of the third singer induced Gazzaniga to give one of the *prime buffe a vicenda* a double role (Donna Anna and Maturina) and to create for the third the new, insignificant charac-ter of Donna Ximena.[26] A notable consequence is that Donna Anna disappears completely from the plot after the dramatic opening scenes, and with her Don Ottavio also almost completely disappears, a part that was sung by Antonio Baglioni, the same tenor who in the following autumn would create the role of Don Ottavio in Mozart's opera in Prague.[27] Bertati also took from Molière the episode in which Don Giovanni seeks to silence Biagio's jealousy by beating him up, as well as the scene in which the protagonist skillfully interposes himself between two women giving each to believe that the other is mad (but whereas in Molière it involves two peasant girls, here it involves Maturina and Donna Elvira); in the end, the final visit that Donna Elvira pays Don Giovanni faithfully reproduces Molière's Act IV, scenes vi and vii. An innovation with respect to the tradition as far back as Tirso is the elimination of the double banquet with the statue; however, we cannot call the drinking songs to the city of Venice and its ladies innovations,[28] neither are the buffooneries of the final scene, because they were probably already customary for the commedia dell'arte.

The plot of Bertati's libretto is certainly the most direct prece-dent for the libretto Da Ponte provided Mozart. In the first scene, Don Giovanni's servant (who here goes by the name Pasquariello) strolls in the dark in a garden, grumbling to himself about his master, who "having been charmed by Donna Anna, / has furtively introduced himself there; / while I, on the lookout perfectly silent and still, / Must attend him here." Upon hearing a noise, he hides himself; it is Don Giovanni followed by Donna Anna, who wants to discover who he is, but who retires upon the Commendatore's arrival. There follows a brief duel (scene ii), and the Commendatore is quickly wounded; his laments alternate with the voices of Don Giovanni and Pasquariello, sometimes singly, sometimes together, until the laments cease, and Don Giovanni, cutting short his servant's remonstrances, leaves with him. From the house, Duke Ottavio and Donna Anna now exit, followed by servants with torches; at the sight of her father's corpse, Donna Anna faints, then, barely revived, tells her fiancé of being surprised in her apartment by an unknown man who tried to take advantage of her. Ottavio burns with indignation and declares he is certain the evildoer will be discovered and punished; meanwhile he exhorts her to find solace "in a husband's love," but she declares her intention of retiring to a convent "as long as her father / remains unavenged" (and thus is established a relationship between the two absolutely similar to the one established in Da Ponte's libretto). Donna Anna leaves, and, before following her, Ottavio remains onstage (scene iv) to sing his only aria, "I hoped the moment was near / Of entering safe port; / but hardly had I sighted shore, / than I return to the high seas." Donna Anna disappears definitively, thus leaving to Donna Elvira the principal female role; Ottavio will return briefly to dictate the inscription for the Commendatore's statue and to participate in the buffoonery of the final scene.

Scene v carries us to a place in the countryside "outside the walls of Villena" amidst rustic abodes and a noble villa (Villena is the town in Aragon where all the action unfolds); Pasquariello makes new remonstrances to Don Giovanni, who elatedly announces to him that he has left the city in order to meet Donna Ximena who awaits him "in order to be able to speak to [him] / with greater freedom." A lady arrives in a carriage, and he sets about observing her: it is Donna Elvira (scene vi) who immediately introduces herself in an aria "Povere femmine," in which she accuses all men of being inconstant and untrustworthy. In recitative, she then says that she is in search "of the unfaithful husband, / who after swearing his faith to me / left me abandoned after three days." Don Giovanni, who had not recognized her at first and had approached her, now moves quickly to avoid her reproaches, leaving to Pasquariello the job of providing her with an explanation. Embarrassed, the servant, like Molière's Sganarelle, drawns upon the figure of Alexander the Great (scene vii): Don Giovanni, he says, is the Alexander the Great of women; and here is the list of his conquests (in an aria and in "a list of several arm-lengths"): "in Italy / I have written down over a hundred. / In France and Spain / There are I don't know how many . . . ." Donna Elvira angrily chases him away, remains alone (scene viii) for a brief recitative and then exits, leaving the stage free for Don Giovanni and Donna Ximena. He swears he wants to marry her as quickly as possible, "but a certain matter / obliges me to my utmost regret / to defer the wedding for a few days." Donna Ximena reveals she is jealous, and Don Giovanni reassures her with an aria that begins "Because of you / I will not even look other women in the face," but he concludes in an aside to the audience "I also intend to enter this one's name into the catalogue." He leaves her alone to recite four lines before she also exits (scene x).

A new change of set is unnecessary: from the rustic houses come Maturina, "Maturina's peasant husband" Biagio, and peasants "playing castanets" (scene xi). The wife, Maturina, sings two short strophes to which all respond with singing and dancing; Pasquariello arrives and taking the wife's hand sings the third strophe; the peasants depart, except for Biagio who protests against Pasquariello. Don Giovanni arrives (scene xii), intervenes in the dispute and boxes Pasquariello's ears; Biagio laughs but quickly stops when Don Giovanni in turn caresses Maturina and pays her compliments; he protests and is beaten (while Pasquariello laughs);

he sings the aria "A me schiaffi sul mio viso!" and is chased away. Maturina makes as if to follow him (scene xiii), but she lets herself be stopped by new compliments from Don Giovanni; she affirms "I am ashamed / to hear myself speaking tenderly / when there is someone else hearing everything I say"; to comply Pasquariello leaves, and she puts up hardly any opposition to Don Giovanni (scene xiv). The latter swears "by heaven" he wants to marry her, and she "begins to believe / what you tell me; / and from this moment / I also feel I am falling in love in you." After the aria "If you make me worthy / to enjoy such an honor, / I will be yours, sir, / and will love you with all my heart . . ." they enter her house together.

Scenes xv through xviii also take place in view of the villa and the rustic houses. While Pasquariello contemplates leaving Don Giovanni's service, he is approached by Donna Ximena who has begun to have her doubts. Don Giovanni comes on and quickly finds he has to juggle three women: he sends Donna Ximena home; alone with Maturina and Donna Elvira, he makes each believe that the other is mad and leaves them at grips with one another in a duet in which they mock each other in turn. With scene xix we are transferred to a "remote place surrounded by cypresses" with a tomb and the equestrian statue of the Commendatore, at which an engraver is working on an inscription dictated by Don Ottavio (we will see it already finished in the next scene). Before leaving, Ottavio also has threatening words for the murderer who "if he can hide / from human justice, / will not escape the sovereign anger of heaven." The guilty man is soon within easy reach along with Pasquariello (scene xx) whom he asks: "What's wrong if I come / to see for sport / whether he's at home here, now that he's dead?" He laughs at the inscription that has just been finished ("On him who dragged me to an evil death, / I here await my vengeance from heaven") and jokingly orders Pasquariello to invite the statue to dinner. Thus begins a duet in which the servant, who reluctantly obeys, indicates that the statue has nodded its head. Don Giovanni does not believe him and repeats the invitation: "I invite you to dinner, Commendatore, / if you will do me the honor. / Will you come?" The statue also answers him with an absurdity: "I will come."

In Don Giovanni's house (scene xxi), while a servant sets the table for dinner, Donna Elvira arrives. Don Giovanni invites her to stay (scene xxii), but her feelings have changed and she has only come to ask him to change his way of life; she is angered that Don Giovanni derides her with hurried courtesies, and therefore leaves after having sung the aria "I am no longer your wife, / extinguished is the flame in me." Don Giovanni (scene xxiii), for whom the fact of no longer being loved has "almost reawakened in his breast / the remains of his old affection," sits down to dinner, and torments the starving Pasquariello who has already placed a croquette in his mouth and is listening to an instrumental concert. Finally allowed at the table, Pasquariello wants something to drink, but must first sing a drinking song in praise of Venice and its ladies (with this the finale begins); he does this in two arias in a row, but then there is knocking at the door and the two servants (there is another one, Lanterna, who has only a few bars to sing)[29] go to open the door and return filled with fear. Don Giovanni then goes and is amazed to encounter the statue; he admits him and invites him to dine (scene xxiv), but the Commendatore admonishes him: "He who has left this mortal coil / Does not eat vile food. / Another end leads me here, / Other than dining"; the trembling Pasquariello is ordered to have the playing and singing continue. The Commendatore invites both of them to dinner ("No" from Pasquariello) and asks that Don Giovanni give him his hand as a pledge of acceptance; it is an icy grip, but Don Giovanni stubbornly refuses to repent, and the scene transforms itself into hell; "only the forward wings remain, whither Pasquariello has fled in terror." Surrounded by furies, Don Giovanni drowns with horrible laments, and everything returns to its former state for the last scene.

Now only five characters burst onto the stage: Donna Elvira, Donna Ximena, Duke Ottavio, Maturina and Lanterna; Pasquariello has remained there from the preceding scene, and of the other two, Donna Anna has ceded to Maturina the singer who played her role, and Biagio has not had time to take off the statue's costume. In Pasquariello's confused narration the only thing that is clear is that Don Giovanni "with ugly hobgoblins / descended to hell." Everyone is surprised ("ecstatic"), but they quickly decide:

Più non facciasi parola del terribile successo,	Let us no longer speak Of the terrible things that have happened.
ma pensiamo invece adesso di poterci rallegrar . . . . Che potressimo mai far?	Let us now think instead Of how to cheer ourselves up . . . . What could we do?
Donne A a a, io vò cantare: io vo mettermi a saltar.	*Ladies* Ah, ah, ah, I want to sing. I want to jump up and down.
Don Ottavio La Chitarra io vò suonare.	*Don Ottavio* I want to play the guitar.
Lanterna Io suonar vò Contrabasso.	*Lanterna* I want to play the double bass.
Pasquariello Ancor io per far del chiasso il fagotto vò suonar.	*Pasquariello* To make some noise I want to play the bassoon.

Don Ottavio	*Don Ottavio*
Tren, tren, trinchete, trinchete trè.	Tinkle, tinkle, tinkle.
Lanterna	*Lanterna*
Flon, flon, flon, flon, flon, flon, flon.	Flon, flon, flon, flon, flon, flon, flon.
Pasquariello	*Pasquariello*
Pu, pu, pu, pu, pu, pu, pu.	Pu, pu, pu, pu, pu, pu, pu.
Tutti	*All*
Che bellissima pazzia!	What lovely craziness!
Che stranissima armonia!	What harmony most strange!
Così allegri si va a star.	Thus let us all be happy!

The final verses carry to the point of absurdity the puppet-like psychology of the characters and indulgence toward facile buffoonery that occasionally characterize Bertati's libretti. One must recognize the theatrical intuition demonstrated in the efficacious cut of several scenes (especially the opening ones) and the cunning ability to furnish the necessary supports for the composer's task. Noteworthy among the many restagings of Gazzaniga's single act is the one for London in 1794, which is entitled "*Il Don Giovanni*, a tragi-comic Opera in one act. The Music by Messrs. Gazzaniga, Sarti, Federici, and Guglielmi. The words are new, by L. da Ponte, poet of this theater, except those that are not marked with inverted commas"; in the event, even though there are many changes (among others, with regard to tragedy, the introduction of a chorus and a funeral march, and with regard to comedy, the reuse of Leporello's catalogue aria), many of Bertati's scenes remain, including the final whirling laughter. Among the new items is a drinking song by Don Giovanni "to the city / that having traveled everywhere / we have found to be the best," a city that turns out to be "my great city of London."[30]

The unevenness in Gazzaniga's score suggests that Bertati applied his abilities to allow the composer to reuse music he had composed for earlier occasions. Certain arias with a generic literary and musical quality may have lent themselves to such an end, arias with pleasing singing melodies, which, however, lack specific expressive characteristics closely connected to a particular character or situation. For example, Duke Ottavio's single aria, "Vicin sperai l'istante" (scene iv), of moderate virtuosity and almost in the style of *opera seria*;[31] Donna Elvira's first aria, "Povere femmine" (scene vi), in which she philosophizes on women's destiny and men's inconstancy, but does not seem particularly disturbed by the difficulty of her own situation; and perhaps also Don Giovanni's aria, "Per voi nemmeno in faccia" (scene ix), divided into two parts (Andante espressivo in 2/4 and Allegretto in 3/4), although the second part depicts the character's duplicity well enough, in promising fidelity while he thinks to himself of his list of conquests.[32] It is almost certain that Pasquariello's drinking song, "A Venezia singolar," stems from the score of *Antigono*, which Gazzaniga had written for Rome in 1779.[33]

The idea of performing *Don Giovanni* as the second act of *Il capriccio drammatico* spared the composer the task of writing an overture. The ambiguity between an opera unto itself and an opera within an opera (which in order to be realistic would have also required an overture of its own) was resolved in favor of the second alternative by having the curtain rise directly upon the introduction. In this regard, I wonder if Gazzaniga, who had not only been trained in Naples but had also maintained frequent connections with its theaters,[34] had come to know Tritto's opera, which in choosing to contain so much material within a single act constituted the single and most immediate antecedent of his own opera. It is certain that, like Tritto, he chose for his introduction the key of E-flat major, and used it to establish a nocturnal atmosphere—in

Tritto as background to the chatter between Don Giovanni and Pulcinella, in Gazzaniga as background to the soliloquizing of Pasquariello bemoaning his fate. Analogous also is the choice of a movement in moderate tempo (in Tritto Andantino, in Gazzaniga Moderato), and analogous the tonal planning whereby, after a series of modulations, the end returns to the opening key (in Tritto in the major mode for Donna Anna's aria, in Gazzaniga in the minor mode for the death of the Commendatore). Gazzaniga's introduction has for some time attracted the attention of scholars because of the suggestions it may have offered for the fiery beginning of Mozart's opera. I too admit that Mozart may have known it and that something of it may have remained in his mind, for example, the chords of B flat and F on which Don Giovanni and Donna Anna begin their bitter altercation;[35] but in their overall continuity and excitement they both form part of the traditions of comic opera to which both settings belong. While in *opera seria*, at least through Gluck, the interest was principally concentrated on the arias (the lyric moments that followed each advance in the action), the principal direction of comic opera was toward movement and suggesting varied attitudes, an aim that was sharpened in the most interesting moments of the action, the introduction and the finales, which came to be conceived as complex musical unities, held together, even in the course of continually evolving action, by constant references to a central key.[36] Mozart had made this tradition his own, intensifying it and renewing it in *Le nozze di Figaro* to the point of drawing it out to a large-scale continuity that embraced the development of each of the acts; even if he had not known Gazzaniga's precedent, he would have had to continue in this direction in his new opera.

Gazzaniga also begins well. His introduction, though shorter, makes a marked impression through its rapid transition (sustained by an uninterrupted rhythmic continuity)[37] from the comic situation of the servant who fumes and mumbles, to the duel and the Commendatore's death. It begins, as I have already mentioned, in E-flat major, with a beautiful phrase in the strings continued in the oboes and concluding with a soft horn call; immediately afterward a quiver of impatience anticipates the twittering of Pasquariello's protests, which forms the basis for a rhythmic continuity that proceeds uninterruptedly in the altercation between Don Giovanni and Donna Anna, alternating invectives that soon pass from a duet to a trio through the comments that Pasquariello adds from his hiding place. The aforementioned chords of B-flat and F above which the altercation takes place form a natural bridge to the modulation to the dominant that carries the piece forward; thus a natural resolution occurs with the return of E-flat at the moment of Donna Anna's flight and the arrival of the Commendatore, whose light Don Giovanni, in a traditional gesture, extinguishes with his sword. Quick, new modulations accompany the duel, but the tonic now returns, in the minor, the instant the Commendatore is wounded, and then insistently in the minor mode (with a few excursions to other keys) until the closing measures in which the laments of the dying man are echoed by the oboes. The piece is thus rendered coherent through the constructive tonal planning as well as through the continuity of the flexible rhythm, and particularly in the continual transformation through accents dictated by the syllabic declamatory style of the voices and through sonorities created by the orchestra, but not through themes that have a definite melodic and rhythmic configuration. And its impetus is more short-winded than Mozart's realization of the analogous situation, which will add almost immediately the trembling duet in which Donna Anna will demand and obtain a vow of vengeance.

Here also, as later in Mozart, the sudden movement to recitative between Don Giovanni and Pasquariello creates an effective contrast between drama and sinister buffoonery; but then the recitative draws itself out without any reprise of the musical interest in the scenes between Donna Anna and Duke Ottavio. Thus begins the succession of extended recitatives and relatively brief lyric pieces that will characterize the opera, pieces that are, to be sure, pleasingly singable but lacking any expressive intensity to mark the particular character's situation. (This may have arisen from the necessity of condensing so much material.) Thus Donna Elvira's aria in scene vi, although labeled "cavatina" in the score does not have any of the introspective qualities with which a cavatina often introduces a character to the audience. Neither does she fare any better in the duet in the next scene, when she inserts her own annoyed interjections or comments to herself ("My jealous heart / Is tearing itself apart") during the impetuous rhythms of Pasquariello's enumeration of the famous list. Donna Ximena is presented only in recitative and as reflected in the seduction aria that Don Giovanni sings to her; later she will reappear briefly in two recitative dialogues, the second of which, with Donna Elvira, is a bland duplication of the bickering duet that follows almost immediately between Donna Elvira and Maturina; she returns at the end to participate in the buffoonery of the final scene. A superfluous character, introduced for who knows what reason (already her equivalent in Act I of *Il capriccio drammatico* had almost disappeared after having sung one comic aria) does not even have an aria here.

The piece with which Maturina and Biagio introduce themselves is also labeled "cavatina with chorus" and quickly highlights their rustic background with the tarantella rhythm (alternating between Larghetto in minor and Allegro in major). But the two strophes that she sings, and that the chorus answers by dancing to the same music, do not tell us anything else about her; especially since the same music also serves for a third strophe for Pasquariello, who "chases among the peasants, takes Maturina by the hand, and dances with her." Biagio, who so far has only taken part in the chorus, protests in recitative, in which he unwisely sends home the peasants who could have backed him up; so much the worse for him, since Don Giovanni now enters to pay court to Maturina (Pasquariello who had first boasted that "I am a noble cavalier, I am . . . Don Giovannino," now quickly draws back: "I bow to the greater man"), and by striking Biagio gives him the opportunity to sing his own aria, "A me schiaffi sul mio viso," a typical comic aria for the most part parlante in which most of his indignation is directed toward Maturina ("To your mother, to your aunt, / to your grandmother I now go. / I will tell all your relatives / what you have done") and toward Pasquariello, who laughs. Don Giovanni and Maturina are left alone (scene xiv), and the seduction rapidly leads to Maturina's aria "Se pur degna voi me fate / di goder d'un tanto onore, / sarò vostro, o mio Signore, / e di core v'amerò" ["If you indeed make me worthy / To enjoy such an honor, / I will be yours, oh my lord, / And with all my heart will love you."], first Andantino affettuoso and then Allegro, which is the third opportunity for this singer to show the various dramatic stances she could assume (she had first played the role of Donna Anna) and to confirm Gazzaniga's facility with non-dramatic, yet persuasive and caressing expressions.

Maturina will again take part in scene xviii in the comic duet with Donna Elvira where she gives voice to Gazzaniga's other vein, that of comic pieces that are free and easy, if not particularly memorable, to which also belongs the duet between Don Giovanni and Pasquariello before the Commendatore's equestrian statue (which then briefly becomes a trio through the latter's intervention). And the other diva, Donna Elvira, will have another cantabile aria when she appears in Don Giovanni's house to make her last remonstrances. Then the story will turn toward its end with Pasquariello's drinking songs and the brief disturbance brought on by the apparition of the statue and the "transformation of the scene into hell," returning to the comic tone more familiar to Gazzaniga in the incongruous finale.

An acclaimed composer with notable success in his own day, Gazzaniga should be studied on the basis of some of his better operas. He probably does not present himself at his best with the music for Bertati's patchwork libretto, which fortuitously has attracted our attention; even taking into account the success of the opening sequence of scenes in his opera does not suffice to confirm the importance that has been granted him as the precursor of, and not simply the temporal antecedent to, Mozart.

CHAPTER FOUR: MOZART AND DA PONTE: AN ALMOST NEW KIND OF SPECTACLE

1. The Meeting of Composer and Librettist

Beethoven's harsh judgement of Mozart's *Don Giovanni*, which he considered scandalous, was undoubtedly a reflection of his high artistic pretensions and uncompromising morals. Nevertheless, it may also reflect an aristocratic Viennese prejudice against a plot which was already discredited in and of itself, which moreover was treated by a librettist and composer neither of whom had ever achieved full social acceptance in the capital of the Habsburg empire: a librettist and composer who were very different from one another yet ideally matched to create a series of masterpieces.

Music was the center of Mozart's brief life (Salzburg, 27 January 1756–Vienna, 5 December 1791) from his first lessons with his father at the age of four, his first short pieces composed at the age of five and his debut as a performer at the age of six together with his sister, who was five years older. Fortunately, the zeal with which Leopold Mozart—himself a violinist, composer, and the author of a treatise on violin playing—nurtured his son's precocious talent did not harm Wolfgang Amadeus's musical development; one wonders how much the father's vigilant and yet affectionate concern (which was exercised, even when the son was not in his presence, with letters and requests for letters) influenced his maturation or lack thereof with regard to nonmusical aspects of his personality. However, the young prodigy's truly exceptional musical sensibility, facility, and memory effortlessly survived his demanding apprenticeship and profited from the many musical encounters and experiences. Neither did he lack for warmth within his family circle, as is documented by the dedication of a father who subordinated his own career to the superior gifts he recognized in his son.[1]

Mozart's musical output embraced the most amazing variety of genres and media, vocal and instrumental, sacred and profane, for chamber and orchestra, with a confidence and fluency that have come to define the distinctive characteristics of his universal genius. He was also exceptional in his operatic activity, but because in this field he had to depend on commissions from courts or theaters his operatic activity was intermittent. Already at the age of twelve, in 1768, he had composed, in hopes of a production in Vienna, the *dramma giocoso La finta semplice* [The Pretended Simpleton] (to a libretto by Marco Coltellini). In the event, this his first operatic composition was performed in 1769 in Salzburg, a year after his one-act singspiel *Bastien und Bastienne* had already been performed privately in Vienna.[2] Travels in Italy (which alternated with brief returns to Salzburg) resulted in two *opere serie*, *Mitridate re di Ponto* and *Lucio Silla* (Milan, 1770 and 1772), along with the serenade *Ascanio in Alba* (Modena, 1771), for which Giuseppe Parini wrote the text;[3] but after returning to Salzburg, Mozart had no further opportunities to write for the theater until 1774, when he received a commission from the Munich court for

La finta giardiniera [The Gardener in Disguise] another *dramma giocoso*, whose text was originally by Ranieri de' Calzabigi, once again revised by Coltellini.[4] Also for Munich, after a gap of several years, was the production of *Idomeneo re di Creta* in 1781, the first opera in which Mozart, now completely cognizant of his own creative and dramatic needs, succeeded in imposing his ideas upon his librettist Giambattista Varesco.

His transfer to Vienna in the summer of 1781 should have offered him more frequent opportunities to write for the theater. But instead, after the three-act singspiel *Belmont und Constanze oder die Entführung aus dem Serail* [Belmont and Constanze, or The Abduction from the Seraglio] (produced in 1782), it was not until February 1786 that he succeeded in having another opera staged, in this instance his other one-act Singspiel, *Der Schauspiel-direktor* [The Impresario], which was performed in the park of Schönbrunn. Between these two works were two unfinished projects both of them comic, *L'oca del Cairo* [The Goose of Cairo] and *Lo sposo deluso* [The Deluded Bridegroom] Nothing would have indicated that he was so close to an explosion of his enormous talent as a composer of opera (only in part thanks to Vienna).

The librettist of *Lo sposo deluso* was long thought to have been the Venetian adventurer and man of letters Lorenzo Da Ponte, who, a few years older than Mozart (he was born in 1749 in Ceneda, known today as Vittorio Veneto), would later end his long and often troubled life in New York in 1838.[5] Originally named Emanuele Conegliano, he assumed the name of the bishop of Ceneda upon being baptized, along with his father and two brothers, when the family converted from Judaism to Catholicism. As a seminarian in Portogruaro, he took minor orders in 1770 and taught there, becoming vice-rector and an ordained priest in 1773. Later he taught in Treviso, but was banished in 1776 for having written a treatise inspired by Rousseau; a libertine in his conduct as well as his ideas, he was forced by an accusation of adultery in 1779 to flee Venice also, a city where he had come to know Casanova and Gasparo Gozzi, among other notables. In 1782, after eventful sojourns in Gorizia and Dresden, he finally landed in Vienna and succeeded in 1783, through the support of Metastasio and Salieri, in being named "poet of the imperial theaters."

Up to this point, Da Ponte had not numbered among his various literary activities any experience as a librettist, so that his first libretti for Salieri, Martin y Soler, and Gazzaniga were not exactly successes. Furthermore, he encountered difficulties with another, more mature man of letters with greater expertise in the theater, the *abate* Giambattista Casti. Da Ponte was, however, a cultured man with a sharp mind and notable resources, and quickly applied himself to acquiring the necessary experience, ready to highlight his best qualities in his intense collaboration with Mozart. After Mozart's death, he did not long remain imperial poet because his intrigues in favor of his mistress the soprano Adriana Ferraresi Del Bene, and the death of his patron Joseph II led to his dismissal. Of the many years that remained of his life, those spent in London from 1793 to 1805 were no less adventurous; there also he was employed as a librettist and theatrical impresario. He had, however, established, if not a marriage, at least a stable union that put an end to his career as a libertine, a career that has elicited comparisons with Casanova. In 1805, to escape his creditors he set sail for America. Forced to support a family by a variety of odd jobs, he exploited opportunities to give lessons in Italian literature and propagandize for its classics; he ended up teaching at Columbia University in New York.

Alfred Einstein astutely pointed out two operatic events that both Mozart and Da Ponte witnessed and that, as representative indications of the evolution of the concept of comic opera, help to explain the birth of *Le nozze di Figaro* and *Don Giovanni*: they are the Viennese productions of *Il re Teodoro in Venezia* (1784, libretto by Casti and music by Giovanni Paisiello) and *La villanella rapita* [The Abducted Country Girl] (1785, libretto by Giovanni Bertati and music by Francesco Bianchi), two operas rich in characters and situations that show how the genre was distancing itself from its customary levity.[6] With these precedents, Mozart and Da Ponte, each desirous of calling attention to himself within the Viennese theater milieu, set about collaborating on *Le nozze di Figaro* animated with the idea of doing something new.

That this did indeed involve a true collaboration between librettist and composer is documented in Da Ponte's brief preface to the libretto. He first defines his "*commedia per musica* taken from the French" as "an imitation, or rather an extract" of his model, *La Folle journée ou Le Mariage de Figaro* by Beaumarchais, a model that was making a great stir at the time having finally reached the stage only in 1784.[7] Da Ponte then warns that, even though he had suppressed one entire act of the original and reduced the number of characters, "the opera will not be among the shortest, . . . for which reason *we* hope that the variety of threads woven through the plot will suffice as an excuse, . . . and *the multiplicity of musical pieces that had to be written* . . . to express precisely the diverse passions with diverse colors . . . and *our* desire, particularly, to offer *an almost new kind of spectacle*."[8] This is a self-conscious and self-satisfied text that beginning in the first person singular quickly passes to the plural after having mentioned "all the study, diligence, and care of the *maestro di Cappella* [i.e., the composer] and me." Unfortunately, this clear evidence of collaboration finds no verification in Mozart's correspondence, which is curiously full of lacunae during this period;[9] thus we must content ourselves with vague hints provided once more by Da Ponte in his late *Memorie* in which, despite his eagerness to document above all how he himself contributed to overcoming the difficulties imposed against the performance, he deigns to recognize that the initiative stemmed from the composer:

> As to the first [i.e., Mozart, the first of two dear friends who had asked him to provide a libretto], I easily conceived that the immensity of his genius demanded an extended subject, multiform, sublime. Conversing with him one day on this matter, he asked me if I could easily reduce to the dimensions of an opera Beaumarchais' comedy entitled *Le nozze di Figaro*. I liked the proposal and promised him I would do it.[10]

Le nozze di Figaro had it premiere at the Burgtheater in Vienna on 1 May 1786 and enjoyed moderate success. It was performed several more times, but soon the new opera by Da Ponte's other "friend," *Una cosa rara* by Martin y Soler, also to a libretto by Da Ponte, directed the attention of the Viennese elsewhere.[11] As a compensation, the opera enjoyed a great success in December of that same year in Prague, where it was restaged by the company of the impresario Pasquale Bondini; Mozart, who had gone to Prague to supervise its preparation, wrote to a friend beaming with happiness: "Here they speak of nothing but *Figaro*; they don't play or whistle or sing anything except *Figaro*. They go to no opera other than *Figaro*, eternally *Figaro*."[12] Returned to Vienna, the next February, he had in his pocket a contract for a new opera to be given in Prague the following winter.

2. The Birth of Dramma Giocoso in Don Giovanni

Mozart and Da Ponte may have been oriented toward choosing the subject of the punished rake through their more or less direct contact with two artists who had already taken part in operatic incarnations of the old myth. One of these artists is Vincenzo Righini, the author of *Il convitato*, which had been staged in Prague eleven years earlier; Da Ponte had written a libretto for him also, *Demogorgone, o sia Il filosofo confuso* [Demogorgone, or The Confused Philosopher] which had been produced in Vienna in the summer of 1786. The other was the mezzo soprano Celeste Coltellini, who performed the role of Lesbina (Pulcinella's fiancée and another object of Don Giovanni's attention) in the Neapolitan production of Lorenzi and Tritto's *Convitato* in 1783. Coltellini (the daughter of the librettist with whom Mozart had already collaborated twice) often appeared in Vienna, where she had sung in *La villanella rapita* among other works;[13] for the Viennese production of *La villanella rapita* Mozart had composed two additional ensembles in which she took part. But the basic element in the choice must have been the desire on the part of both the poet and the musician to find a subject that would equal in quality the elements that contributed most to the extraordinary success of *Le nozze di Figaro* in Prague—a subject that through a vertiginous sequence of events and surprises could resemble the characteristics that had induced Beaumarchais to give as the first title of his comedy *Les folles journées*. Among the many versions of the myth of Don Giovanni there was never any lack of variety of characters and episodes, nor of urgent rhythm in the action; on the contrary, from the hypertrophic three *jornadas* of Tirso's *Burlador* stems the "vastness and grandeur" that each new version tried to select from and curtail. The variety in social class, temperament, and motivation among the characters lent itself to the "multiplicity of musical pieces" that would express "precisely the diverse passions with diverse colors"; it even extended the scale to include murderous violence and the awesome final punishment. It was more difficult to equal *Le nozze* with regard to topicality of subject matter and social relevance; but the suppression of the antecedent Neapolitan action (with its attendant flight and shipwreck), of the interventions at the Spanish court, and of the appearances of the victims before that court, the "young, extremely licentious cavalier" (as Don Giovanni is described in the libretto) lost every vestige of historical reference and returned to the sphere of every-day reality for the audience of the day. Another contributing factor is the reduction of the spatial context to a single "city in Spain," indeed to a single quarter that encompasses the palaces of Don Giovanni and the Commendatore (who here is simply Donna Anna's father and no more). Even the "village," or "suburb," in which the "peasants" Zerlina and Masetto live is "contiguous to Don Giovanni's palace."[14] Thus the critique of the *grand seigneur méchant homme* is brought up to date; and for good measure Mozart adds a gratuitous libertarian sally: the peasants invited to the festivities at Don Giovanni's palace reinforce with martial shouts Don Giovanni's "Viva la libertà," which escaped the mouth of the host with quite a different meaning (not libertarian but libertine).

A letter of Paisiello's (September 1781) containing instructions for a libretto that was to be sent to him in Saint Petersburg from Naples (probably the libretto of *Il barbiere di Siviglia*) suggests to me another factor that may have contributed to the choice of Don Giovanni: "very little recitative, *because they do not understand Italian here*; they want arias, cavatinas, duets, trios, and finales *that occur in the course of the action* in the Neapolitan style."[15] Beyond indicating the newest tendencies in comic opera, Paisiello points to the problem of presenting opera in Italian, a language that was not understood by many in either Saint Petersburg or Prague. Both *Il barbiere* and *Don Giovanni* have extensive recitative, but in both instances (as in *Le nozze di Figaro*) the notoriety of the subject matter minimized the difficulty.

The attention scholars have paid to Bertati and Gazzaniga's *Don Giovanni* as the direct predecessor of Da Ponte and Mozart's therefore appears too exclusive, not to say excessive. The parallels between the text of Act II of *Il capriccio drammatico* produced in Venice in early 1787 and the libretto Da Ponte wrote in the course of the following year (parallels already noted by Friedrich Chrysander) are beyond dispute and most remarkable, but they are insufficient to support Hermann Abert's thesis that the Venetian model determined the choice of subject.[16] To justify his thesis, he points to the presumed brevity of time granted the two authors to create the new opera, which was shorter than that granted for the preparation of *Le nozze* (during which time Mozart also assumed responsibility for preparing performances of *Der Schauspieldirektor*). To me it seems more likely that, having arrived at the decision on the basis of the motives mentioned above, Mozart and especially Da Ponte would be interested in acquainting themselves with the most recent operatic version of the theme they had chosen.[17] Then as now, news of theatrical events transpired rapidly through interested circles, and both Gazzaniga and Bertati were well known in Vienna where the former had sojourned up until a few months before.[18] It was therefore natural for Da Ponte, engaged in working on three different libretti at the same time,[19] not to hesitate to borrow from Bertati's text, both because that was the normal habit in the field of libretto writing, and because he realized he would have to create a substantially new opera because of the many episodes he would have to add to those he was able to draw from Bertati's single act. This places in a new light Edward Dent's hypothesis that *Don Giovanni*, like *Le nozze di Figaro*, was originally intended to be divided into four acts.[20]

Mozart, not Da Ponte, probably thought of adopting from Bertati's model the rapid opening sequence that blazes through the first two scenes (to which the third scene with the horror-filled duet between Donna Anna and Don Ottavio is impetuously added on) events that elsewhere (for example, in Tritto's opera) encompassed over half an act. Undoubtedly, he already envisioned the musical and expressive possibilities offered by the rapid transition from the comic monologue of the servant (Leporello/Pasquariello) through the entrance of Don Giovanni and Donna Anna, to the duel and the Commendatore's murder; or those deriving from an ampler long-range plan in which the *dramma giocoso* was framed at each end by the two moments of greatest tragedy, the rake's crime and his punishment from heaven meted out by the victim who acts as heaven's instrument.[21] And from this long-range plan also stems the acceptance of another characteristic derived from Bertati's libretto, the elimination of the lugubrious second scene in the Commendatore's tomb. In the Venetian libretto, the economy imposed by the single act may have been the primary justification for the elimination of this scene; in Mozart's, though it may not have been in Da Ponte's best interest, its elimination was accepted in order not to dilute through repetition the intensity of the finale, repetition which would have been particularly evident because of the earlier spectral admonishment in the cemetery.

Between these two basic elements evidently and intentionally taken from Bertati's libretto (and in some part from Gazzaniga's music), Da Ponte constructed a series of episodes, in part traditional, in part of his own invention, although it is impossible to make absolute statements with regard to novelty in the context of the diffuse and protean tradition of a myth whose ramifications are only partially identifiable. Other correspondences with Bertati are not lacking (the catalogue aria, the invitation addressed to the statue through the frightened servant, and the peasants' wedding songs and dances). Donna Elvira's sudden appearance during Don Giovanni's dinner is, like the entire character, derived from Molière; but in Molière her character is decidedly more pathetic, while the interpretation of Da Ponte and Mozart welds the pathetic to caricature: the repetitiveness with which she intervenes to spoil each of Don Giovanni's new enterprises is decidedly comic; her unintentional adventure with Leporello moves the audience to laugh and feel pity at the same time (this is probably a brilliant invention of Da Ponte's, even though the exchange of clothes is a tradition that goes back to Tirso). Almost completely new, except for some echoes of Goldoni (though fortunately less literary), is Zerlina's role.[22]

Either because Da Ponte was a more hurried and less precise watchmaker than Beaumarchais, or because the more difficult material with its several required passages did not permit him to proceed in a more straightforward manner, the score of *Don Giovanni* is less compact and coherent than that of *Le nozze*. Even if it was first intended to be in four acts, none of them would have had the same unity of action and place as each of the four acts of *Le nozze*; of its two acts, each requires five stage sets, some of which are used only briefly (for example, the graveyard scene, Act II, scene xii, and the scene in Donna Anna's house, Act II, scene xiii).

Scholars have pointed to the designation of the opera as a *dramma giocoso*, interpreting it as an intentional distancing from the common *opere buffe*.[23] In the climate of Romantic and post-Romantic interpretations and interpolations of the opera, emphasizing the most dramatic elements and therefore tending to overlook or minimize the comic elements (or to interpret them in a sinister light), it seemed inconvenient that *Don Giovanni* should have its roots in the humus of a genre that was considered inferior. It was forgotten that among Mozart's operas *La finta giardiniera* and *La finta semplice* were also labelled *drammi giocosi*, and many scholars were unaware that this designation corresponded to a use that had been current in comic libretti for several decades (not to mention

Mozart's colloquial usage of the term *opera buffa* for this opera in his personal catalogue). They failed to take into account that, beyond the already mentioned possibilities, the comic genre offered a vitality that—with the flexibility of its forms, the variety of alternating arias with ensembles, the overwhelming sweep of its finales, and not least the freedom and effectiveness of its expert staging at the hands of the so-called buffo singers—had enriched and enlarged its own expressive possibilities and was ready to welcome the novelties of Mozart's and Da Ponte's opera, a vitality in action and movement that would have been impeded—if not suffocated—in *opera seria* by the rigidity of its conventions.

The cast of *Don Giovanni* (which probably was influenced by the availability of the company that was to stage the work in Prague) also includes the two serious parts and five comic parts of most comic operas. An exception is the Commendatore, who does not have time to assume a character in his first appearance and who returns later as the blind instrument of a higher power, the machine of a *deus ex machina*. Among the actual characters, Donna Anna and Don Ottavio are clearly the two serious roles because of their dignified comportment, an attribute of persons of high rank. At the other extreme of the social order, the label "buffo" is clearly appropriate for the peasants Zerlina and Masetto, and Leporello. Zerlina's rash flirtatiousness, her calculated weakness, and masked moments of strength are beyond a doubt those of the *prima buffa*; and the two men are *buffi caricati*. Leporello is a more mechanical *buffo caricato*, in that the stereotyped mask of the gluttonous and fearful servant is redeemed only through Mozart's musical verve (especially in his opening arietta and in the catalogue aria); less conventional is Masetto with his excessive jealousy, his impotent rebelliousness and his tendency toward self-pity. Finally, Mozart must also have conceived of Donna Elvira as a buffo character, on the borderline between pathos and comedy, passion and compassion, jealousy and abnegation. I would label her a *buffa di mezzo carattere*, were it not for the fact that I have no evidence of female parts that were labeled as such. However, I have some confirmation from Mozart himself; in a letter to his father dated 7 May 1783, he refers to a project for a comic opera in which "it would be necessary to include good female parts of equal importance. One should be *seria*, the other *mezzo carattere*. . . . The third woman can be entirely *buffa*." Thus he anticipates the entire female cast of *Don Giovanni*.[24]

I do not hesitate to attribute to Don Giovanni the label *buffo di mezzo carattere*. His role was so defined in two operas on the same subject, those by Calegari and Guardi. Aside from this, we know that Luigi Bassi, who sang the role in Prague, had a rather high and flexible baritone voice, almost that of a tenor, and that he was consistently praised throughout his successful career for his dramatic intelligence, spirit, and sense of humor, all qualities of a *mezzo carattere*.[25] He had already interpreted such roles in Prague; for example, that of Figaro in *Il barbiere di Siviglia* and of Teodoro in *Il re Teodoro* (both by Paisiello), as well as Count Almaviva in Mozart's *Figaro*, a role that is characterized by the contrast between the aristocratic grandiosity of the feudal lord and the shabby secret vices of the man himself, between his jealous love of the countess and his simultaneous pursuit of other women. Don Giovanni also is a high-ranking gentleman of questionable morals. In order to convey his lack of scruples with respect to women, Mozart had to take advantage of the recognized abilities of Bassi in disguise and dissimulation; for Don Giovanni also is a dissimulator and achieves his greatest comic effects in his professions of love, whose captivating warmth and persuasive sweetness are heard by the audience with full consciousness that they are cold-blooded deceptions. It therefore seems to be beyond doubt that Mozart approached Don Giovanni as a comic character who at times comes particularly close to being a *buffo caricato*—for example, in the Act I quartet, when he tries to make the others believe that Elvira is mad. But as Mozart penetrated the plot with his sharp psychological perception and vivid sense of self-identification, he must have felt that there were other sides to his hero that he could not treat with the same levity as his predecessors had. Not that Mozart and Da Ponte were such severe moralists as to think that eroticism and libertinism were mortal sins; only Don Giovanni's egoism, his damnable, obstinate pride, his extreme contempt for the lives and feelings of others could justify the majesty and anguish of the supernatural act of punishment.

Don Giovanni also had to be a comic opera because that was the type of opera Prague had commissioned from Mozart and because it was his determination to repeat the richness and the success of *Le nozze di Figaro*. Little is known about its period of gestation. Da Ponte claims that *he* first came up with the idea, which Mozart then approved. Here we can believe him because a little earlier in his *Memorie* he gives *Mozart* credit for the idea of using Beaumarchais's play. He goes on to confess that he had to work on three libretti simultaneously.[27] His text certainly shows signs of haste, even with its indisputable excellence of spirit and invention; one example of this is the meeting between Don Giovanni and Leporello in the cemetery (Act II, scene xii)—for the Viennese edition of 1788 it was necessary to add some passages of recitative to explain the stage business of each taking back his own hat and cape, an exchange that Da Ponte had let take place wordlessly in the first version where it is indicated only by a stage direction. Also the number of scene changes could have been reduced, if Da Ponte had had fewer obligations, or if he had not had to follow what were probably interventions by Mozart. The same cannot be said of the score, even though Edward Dent laments, without citing precise instances, that "moments of overwhelming beauty and the greatest dramatic power," stand alongside "curious lapses into the mannerisms of an old-fashioned style, the whole being to some extent marred by a general vagueness and confusion of plan."[28] For the same author, however, the perfection of individual pieces made him mention a moment earlier that "the composer allowed himself a free hand to try experiments in expression and push every technical device to its furthest limits." It must be kept in mind that Mozart's extraordinary natural talents, refined through the long exercise of composing, had conferred upon him an exceptional capacity to develop the creative process in moments of purely mental intense concentration, after which the actual phase of writing unfolded rapidly and with assurance; therefore the account of Mozart's first biographer, Georg Nikolaus Nissen, that Mozart wrote the overture to *Don Giovanni* the night before the dress rehearsal, is worthy of close attention (of course, he must have thought it through before).

In view of his abilities, Mozart probably first developed on his own a particular design for a scene, or particular dramatic effects, and then asked Da Ponte to create the situations and the dramatic developments necessary to realize them. What Mozart wrote in a letter addressed to his father several years earlier, during the preparation of *Die Entführung aus dem Serail,* should be viewed in this light: "in an opera, poetry must be the completely devoted daughter of music."[29] The sentences that immediately follow clarify the meaning of this statement, which at first may appear disconcerting: he maintains that "music totally dominates and makes one forget all else," so that "an opera should be all the more pleasing in which the plot is well developed but the words are written only with the music in mind without insertions here and there for the sake of rhyme or of words or entire strophes that ruin the intention of the composer."

In September 1787, when Mozart arrived in Prague to preside over the production of the opera, it is said that aside from the overture he still had left to compose Masetto's aria "Ho capito, signor sì" (Act I, scene viii), and the duet between Don Giovanni and Leporello at the beginning of Act II and the second finale. The opera, which was announced for a gala on 4 October in honor of an archducal couple passing through Prague, was not yet ready and had to be replaced by a restaging of *Le nozze di Figaro*. In the event, *Don Giovanni* was performed with extraordinary success on 29 October (even before the work began, Mozart was greeted with a triple "hurrah" upon his appearance in the orchestra)[30] and after numerous performances in Prague was taken to Leipzig and other German cities by the same company. In Vienna, however, where it was performed in May 1788 at the Burgtheater with—at least in part—better singers, it enjoyed only a modest reception.[31] On this occasion, Don Ottavio's aria "Il mio tesoro" (Act II, scene x), which did not suit the tenor, was cut, and the tenor was given instead a new aria, "Dalla sua pace" (Act I, scene xiv) (today both lovely arias are usually performed); two new scenes were added after Act II, scene x, for Zerlina and Leporello (usually omitted today), and a fourth for Donna Elvira (today performed as Act II, scene xi, including an accompanied recitative and the aria "Mi tradì quell'alma ingrata"). The final scene was also suppressed and instead the remaining characters all return to the stage to witness Don Giovanni's disappearance into the abyss and thereupon emit a scream of horror and astonishment. The opera was set aside after fifteen performances (fewer than normal), but beginning in 1789 was restaged in various other cities, which often performed the work in German translation.

Chapter Five: Mozart's *Don Giovanni*

As with Beaumarchais's *La Folle journée ou Les Noces de Figaro*, the alternative title of Mozart's *Il dissoluto punito ossia Il Don Giovanni* prevailed over the main title. But perhaps it should also have had some expression to remind one of the protagonist's "folles nuitées," his mad and maddening nights. How many such nights there were—at least two, perhaps three—is difficult to say, since temporal indications in Da Ponte's libretto are unclear, but it is indisputable that their heady excitement found a parallel in the pressing urgency of Mozart's music, which I will now describe scene by scene. My reading will be much more rapid and succinct than the more detailed one by Massimo Mila referred to in my preface and the many others that have preceded it over the course of two centuries of critical discussion and investigation of this opera,[1] but I hope that it will serve to inspire the reader to listen to Mozart's masterpiece again and again.

1. The Overture

The opera begins with an overture in D major, the same key as the overture to *Le nozze di Figaro*, and is similarly in the form of the first movement of a symphony.[2] The instrumental forces include, aside from the usual strings, two flutes, two oboes, two clarinets in A, two bassoons, two horns in D, two trumpets in D, and timpani (D-A)—an orchestra of the same size as that of Mozart's mature symphonies. The overture begins with an introduction in a moderate tempo (Andante) and in the minor mode anticipating in altered form the theme that will be heard later in the opera when the Commendatore's statue unexpectedly appears in Don Giovanni's home (Act II, scene xvii): two chords for full orchestra separated by tense questioning pauses followed by two long held notes played softly by the woodwinds over chromatically descending chords in the strings, whose rhythm matches the statue's gait. The syncopated figure in the violins, which corresponds to the protagonist's shudder of amazement and his quick recovery, later returns unaltered (except for the adjustments that make up for the absence of voices); in contrast, Mozart condenses and directs toward the central key the theme of Leporello's comic dismay and the tragic ascending and descending scales whose surprising harmonic alterations increase the tension even in the absence of a sonorous crescendo. The foreboding, or predestination, the minor mode, the unstable harmonies, dissolve and then resolve into the gay affirmation of the Allegro molto, solidly in D major.[3] Two brief phrases of unequal length, welded together by a haughty fanfare, the second enriched with tenuous counterpoints from the woodwinds,

constitute the concise first theme. With a figure of staccato repeated notes that move through a crescendo comes the transition to
the second theme. After a brief unison pause on A, the transition
resumes the agitated and voluble tone it began with. After affirm-
ing the key of A major in which the second theme will appear, the
transition expressively deflects the mode toward the minor and
arrives at another resting point on the dominant, E.[4] The second
theme also begins with a brief phrase consisting of two strongly
contrasting elements, each stated twice and then developed further
through canonic repetitions of the first incisive phrase, which
modulates first to a minor, then to C major and then back to a
minor; this first phrase resolves unexpectedly in the key of A
major, which is confirmed by a cadential closing section that constitutes the end of the exposition. The development insistently
uses the exposition's second theme leading it through a series of
modulations; the first theme appears only once, in G major, transformed to g minor after the brief fanfare that connects its two
phrases, and then diverted toward new modulatory elaborations of
the second theme. A pedal on A prepares the retransition of the
development to the third part of the sonata form movement, the
recapitulation. The recapitulation reproduces the first theme and
the first part of the transition through the pause on A; but after
the pause the second part of the transition is taken up again in D
major rather than A major, which then leads to the re-statement
of the second theme and of the closing section in the home key of
D major. However, since Mozart wanted the overture to lead into
the first scene of the opera without a break, he extends the conclusion with a sudden reduction in sonority and a new modulatory
development based on the head motive of the second theme
preparing the key of the first piece in Act I, F major.

2. Act I, Scenes i-iii

Just at the overture moves without interruption into scene i, the next two pieces will also follow each other without pause. The opening comic aria, brief and rapid (Molto allegro), is among the few in the opera with an opening ritornello; Leporello (bass) walks up and down in front of the Commendatore's palace, ruminating in the dark on his discontent ("Notte e giorno faticar") and alternating these ruminations with dreams of grandeur ("Voglio fare il gentiluomo, / e non voglio più servir" ["I would like to be a gentleman; / I no longer want to serve"]). A brief coda to his aria ("Ma mi par che venga gente . . . / non mi voglio far sentir" [But I hear people coming this way . . . / I do not want to be seen"]) shows his pusillanimity; he hides himself in the dark while the orchestra with a crescendo articulates two chords, B-flat and F, which in Gazzaniga's opera also signaled the exit of Don Giovanni (baritone) from the palace, his head buried in his cloak; Donna Anna (soprano) follows, or rather pursues him, trying to hold him back and uncover his face. They melodically lash out at each other in their exchange of invectives, to which are added Leporello's partially ironic, partially fearful comments; their vocal lines intertwine in the repetition of the two opening chords; still anchored in the key of B-flat major, their cadential phrases over Leporello's rapid patter are halted only by a sudden, fortissimo modulation to g-minor and a series of incisive gestures in the double basses, accompanying the entrance of the Commendatore (bass). Donna Anna withdraws to the house, and the exchange of invectives is now taken up by the two men, transformed once more into a trio by

Leporello's invocation: "Potessi almeno / di qui partir!" ["If only / I could leave here!"] After a brief pause, the duel rapidly takes place with urgent runs in the strings, which are finally brought to a halt by a sustained dissonant chord followed by a long pause: the Commendatore falls mortally wounded, and the rhythmic impetus that has been maintained over the course of so many varied events, yields to an Andante, pianissimo, in c minor. In a beautiful passage, to the accompaniment of strings in thirds, are intertwined the disjointed laments of the dying man, Leporello's expressions of amazement and fear, and, with a more full-blown melody, the voice of Don Giovanni, who unexpectedly has his own expressions of sorrow; the trio, to which the timbre of uniformly low voices gives great intensity, transcends the sentiments of the individual characters in a choral contemplation of the solemnity of death.[5]

The voices grow silent, but Mozart once again avoids a break in the music: the series of thirds in the strings accompanies for a few more measures a descending chromatic line in the woodwinds, stated twice and then extinguished on a chord that sounds strangely empty; this is followed by a recitative of sinister whispers in the dark. Leporello is clearly indignant ("Bravo! / Due imprese leggiadre: / sforzar la figlia ed ammazzare il padre!" ["Bravo! / Two easy feats: / To rape the daughter and kill the father!"]), but Don Giovanni, defiant and threatening, silences him and drags him away. An instant later, Donna Anna and Don Ottavio (tenor) exit from the palace accompanied by servants carrying torches. A new recitative is dramatized by agitated figures in the orchestra: at the sight of her father's corpse Donna Anna bursts out with broken phrases alternating with brief punctuations by the woodwinds in surprising modulations; she faints, and it is Don Ottavio's turn to come to her aid and comfort her with equally moving recitative phrases. When she recovers, she believes for a moment she is speaking to her father's murderer: "Fuggi, crudele, fuggi! / lascia

che mora anch'io / ora che è morto o Dio, chi a me la vita diè!"
["Flee, cruel one, flee! / Let me die / Now that the one who gave
me life, O God, is dead!"] This is the beginning of a duet (Allegro)
that returns to the key of the overture, d minor, and proceeds with
a very flexible phrasing, rich modulations, and symphonic development. In the effort to enhearten her, Don Ottavio twice bursts
out with a moving exclamation, varied upon repetition: "Lascia, o
cara, / la rimembranza amara! / hai sposo e padre in me" ["Let go,
oh dear, / Of the bitter memory! / You have a husband and father
in me"]. In a new recitative parenthesis accompanied by the
orchestra (Maestoso, then Adagio), Donna Anna asks and obtains
a solemn oath of vengeance; then the Allegro takes up in phrases
of stupefaction a repeat of the oath, ending with a stretta in which
the voices supplely render the final verses: "tra cento affetti e cento /
vammi ondeggiando il cor" ["Amid a hundred emotions / My
heart is tossing"]. They exit, and the scene changes.

3. Act I, Scenes iv-vi

"A clear evening"; we are on the street. Leporello makes new
remonstrances, at once timid and impudent, to Don Giovanni,
who is on his way to meet a lady, but is distracted by the sight of
another woman and moves aside to watch her. This is Donna
Elvira, "a lady from Burgos abandoned by Don Giovanni" (soprano), who comes upon the stage dressed in traveling clothes (scene
v) and expresses out loud her determination for vengeance in the
aria "Ah! chi mi dice mai" (Allegro in E-flat), preceded by an
orchestral introduction. At the end of each of the two sections that
make up the aria, Don Giovanni and Leporello add their voices,

the one expressing the intention of consoling her, the other the irony of witnessing once again the usual spectacle: "Così ne consolò mille e ottocento." ["Thus he has consoled one thousand eight hundred of them"]. The aria, emphatically dramatic, has a virtuoso coda, at the end of which Don Giovanni moves forward and immediately realizes he has walked into an unhappy situation. In the dialogue that follows, in secco recitative, he finds no other solution to halt the impetus of Donna Elvira's recriminations than to delegate to Leporello the explanation for their departure from Burgos. The servant begins by stammering disconnected phrases; Don Giovanni takes advantage of this diversion to escape, and Leporello finds no other means to console the lady than to pull out his "large book . . . full of the names of Don Giovanni's conquests" and to begin the first part of his famous aria, "Madamina, il catalogo è questo" (Allegro in D major). The enumeration is brazenly comic, with emphatic fermatas on the repeated verse, "Ma . . . in Ispagna son già mille tre" ["But . . . in Spain it's already a thousand three"]; it rests for a moment on the dominant of D (A major) and then passes on to the second part (Andante con moto, in the rhythm of a minuet) in which Leporello reflects with jealous satisfaction upon Don Giovanni's various tastes: "Vuol d'inverno la grassotta, / vuol d'estate la magrotta / . . . Ma passion predominante / è la giovin principiante." ["In winter, he likes them plump, / In summer, thin. / . . . But his greatest passion / Is for the young novice"]. In the end, however, he is not particular "as long as they wear a skirt"; nothing remains for Donna Elvira but to express her bitterness and renewed fury (scene vi) in another secco recitative.

4. Act I, Scenes vii-xv

A new change of scene carries us to "a quarter next to Don Giovanni's palace," where Zerlina (soprano) and Masetto (bass) are celebrating their wedding (scene vii). A piece labeled chorus in the score (Allegro in G major) actually consists of three strophes, one for Zerlina, "Giovinette che fate all'amore," the second for Masetto, "Giovinotti leggeri di testa," and the third for the two of them together; the last verse of each strophe is repeated by two peasant women who are Zerlina's friends, two peasants who are friends of Masetto, and the entire chorus, respectively. As usual, the rhythm is 6/8, but this time it does not bear the stamp of a tarantella. Don Giovanni and Leporello arrive (scene viii, secco recitative) and join the festive group surrounding the bride. Don Giovanni orders Leporello to take everyone to his palace and offer them "chocolate, coffee, wine, and prosciutto," to show them "the garden, gallery, and chambers"; and while they go their way, he holds Zerlina back. Masetto is opposed to this, but Don Giovanni is quick to threaten: "se subito, / senz'altro replicar, non te ne vai, / Masetto, guarda ben, ti pentirai" ["if you / Do not immediately leave without another word, / Watch out, Masetto, you will be sorry"] (he shows him his sword). Masetto is forced to comply in a comic aria of angry submission (Allegro molto in F major): "Ho capito, signor, sì! / Chino il capo e me ne vo" ["I understand, yes, sir! / I bow my head and go"]; under his breath he sings to Zerlina, "Bricconaccia, malandrina / fosti ognor la mia ruina" ["Minx, hussy, / You were ever my ruin"], and "Faccia il nostro cavaliere / cavaliera ancora te." ["May our gentleman / Make a lady of you."] Don Giovanni is finally alone with Zerlina (scene ix) and explains his actions. He begins with adulation: "Vi par che un onest'uomo,

/ un nobil cavalier, qual io mi vanto, / possa soffrir che quel visetto d'oro, / quel viso inzuccherato, / da un bifolcaccio vil sia strapaz-zato?" ["Does it seem right to you that a gentleman, / A noble knight, such as I, / Should suffer seeing your golden little face, / Your sugar sweet face, / Abused by a vile peasant?"] Zerlina at first puts up some opposition but already by the second reply vacillates: "Ah! . . . non vorrei . . . alfine / ingannata restar. Io so che rado / colle donne voi altri cavalieri / siete onesti e sinceri" ["Ah, in the end / I would not like to be deceived. I know that rarely / Are you noblemen / Honest and sincere with women"]; this gives way to Don Giovanni's protests and to his recourse to his final expedient, all the more absurd moments after their first meeting: "in questo istante / io vi voglio sposar . . . / Quel casinetto è mio; soli saremo, / e là, gioiello mio, ci sposeremo" ["This very instant I want to marry you . . . / This little house is mine; we will be alone / And there, my jewel, we will be married"]. Up to this point the recita-tive dialogue has been convincing in its declamation but not in the seduction, even if we grant Zerlina needs little convincing; the magic of the duettino that follows convinces us: "Là ci darem la mano" (Andante in A major). Involved in the action up to this point, Don Giovanni has revealed only arrogance and brutal deci-siveness; he now unfurls in song the caressing and insinuating charm of the seducer. His musical phrase, apparently so simple, is taken up and sweetly prolonged by Zerlina; the modulation to E major renders Don Giovanni's theme more urgent and Zerlina's replies more apprehensive, replies that seem to linger and thus prolong the sweetness of the moment. The first phrase returns, now divided between the two voices, and then the interplay between the increasingly insistent invitations and the dilatory replies is compressed into an ever narrower texture; at the final admission of Zerlina's fragility ("Presto non son più forte" ["Soon I will no longer be strong enough to resist"]), the prevailing tonal stability of the piece (in A major with a brief excursion to E major) gives way to rapid modulations (to f-sharp minor and D major). The final, persuasive invitation and the languidly whispered concession, "Andiam," are taken up again in the closing stretta (Allegro in 6/8) in which the two sing simultaneously, "Andiam, andiam, mio bene, / a ristorar le pene / d'un innocente amor!" ["Let's go, let's go, my beloved, / To restore the pain / Of an innocent love!"]; and thus "they walk toward Don Giovanni's townhouse arm in arm."

The pain was brief and the innocence fragile; but the relief is prevented by the sudden arrival of Donna Elvira (scene x), who "halts Don Giovanni with most desperate gestures" proclaiming, "I am just in time to save this wretched innocent from your barbarous clutches." Don Giovanni tries to resort to a variant of the traditional expedient; he says to Elvira, "Idolo mio, non vedete / ch'io voglio divertirmi?" ["My idol, don't you see / I just wanted to have some fun?"] and to Zerlina, "La povera infelice / è di me innamorata, / e per pietà deggio fingere amore, / ch'io son, per mia disgrazia, uom di buon core" ["The poor girl is in love with me / And out of pity I pretend to love her, / Because I am a good man at heart"]. But Donna Elvira reacts with an energetic aria accompanied by strings alone, "Ah, fuggi il traditore" (Allegro in D major), often labeled Handelian because of its rhythmic and melodic angularity; once finished, she exits "taking Zerlina with her."

Left alone for a few seconds, Don Giovanni is joined by Don Ottavio and Donna Anna (scene xi) and fears for a moment that she suspects him; reassured he professes himself at her service with magniloquent courtesy and has the impudence to ask: "Ma voi, bella Donn'Anna, / perché così piangete? / Il crudele chi fu che osò la calma / turbar del viver vostro?" ["But, fair Donna Anna, / Why do you weep? / Who was so cruel as to dare / To disturb your quiet life?"] Once more the arrival of Donna Elvira interrupts him with a violent apostrophe, "Ah, ti ritrovo ancor, perfido mostro . . ." ["Ah, I find you once more, perfidious monster . . ."], after which recitative gives way to the quartet "Non ti fidar, o misera" (Andante in B-flat major). The melody of Donna Elvira's vocal line is, like all those that mark her character, emphatic and solemn, and it is significant that its closing gesture (almost that of a ceremonial bow) continues and is echoed by the orchestra and in the voices during Donna Anna's and Don Ottavio's suppressed comments ("Cieli, che aspetto nobile, / che dolce maestà!" ["Heavens, what noble demeanor, / What gentle majesty!"]), which take up the second half of the phrase. Don Giovanni will do the same, but the first part of his intervention degrades him even musically to the typical expressions of the comic singer: "La povera ragazza / è pazza, amici miei: / lasciatemi con lei, / forse si calmerà" ["The poor girl / Is mad, my friends. / Leave me alone with her. / Perhaps she will calm down"]. With the two antithetical positions thus established along with those of the as yet undecided listeners, the dispute turns to Donna Elvira's advantage, whose vocal line dominates the other voices with virtuoso flare-ups; Don Giovanni's replies are lost among the signs of growing interest, on the part of Donna Anna and Don Ottavio, in Donna Elvira's situation: "Certo moto d'ignoto tormento / dentro l'alma girare mi sento" ["A certain unknown torment / I feel turning in my soul"]—with an unexpected rhythmic shift to triplets and an augmented fifth chord—"che mi dice per quella infelice / cento cose che intender non sa" ["That tells me of this unfortunate lady / A hundred things my soul does not undertand"]—a complex play of contrapuntal lines, rendered expressive through a half-step descent. A symphonic episode, a phrase of three repeated measures modulating from F major to c minor, to g minor and to B-flat major, separates the voices providing the opportunity for each person to express his or her own state of mind (even that of Don Giovanni who admits to himself that things are going badly); this episode leads to more violent accusations from Donna Elvira: "Mentitore, mentitore, mentitore!" ["Liar!"] Don Giovanni returns in a more excited comic tone ("Zitto! zitto! ché la gente / si raduna a noi d'intorno. / Siate un poco più prudente: / vi farete criticar" ["Hush, hush! / A crowd is gathering. / Be a bit more discreet. / They will criticize you."); but the indomitable Donna Elvira persists. The quartet, by this point a web of various and contrasting exclamations, returns through a long pedal on F to Donna Elvira's opening phrase, thus concluding in her favor. She leaves, and Don Giovanni hastens to follow her, trying first to regain the others' esteem with a gesture of hurried courtesy (in secco recitative): "Perdonate, bellissima Donn'Anna, / se servirvi poss'io, / in mia casa v'aspetto. Amici, addio!" ["Pardon, fairest Donna Anna, / If I can be of service to you, / I await you in my house. Friends, farewell!"]

The orchestra opens scene xiii with a mysterious figure in the cellos and double basses (Allegro assai), followed by an explosion of violent chords from the full orchestra and a scream from Donna Anna, to whom the doubts aroused by Donna Elvira and the sound of Don Giovanni's last words have revealed the truth. Between renewed orchestral outbursts she informs Don Ottavio: "Oh Dei! Quegli è il carnefice / del padre mio . . ." ["Ye gods! He is the murderer / Of my father . . ."], and to his incredulous wonder she begins (above long-held tonic and dominant chords in the orchestra, in e-flat minor, a rare key for Mozart) to recount the events that took place inside the Commendatore's palace at the beginning of the opera;[6] the man wrapped in a cloak "che al primo istante / avea preso per voi: / ma riconobbi poi / che un inganno era il mio . . ." ["whom for an instant, / I mistook for you; / But then I realized / I was deceived . . ."], the struggle in which, almost on the point of succumbing, she recovers her strength and reverses the situation, the pursuit and, finally, the catastrophe the audience has already witnessed. The long, intense recitative accompanied by the orchestra and punctuated by Don Ottavio's anxious exclamations moves without a break into the aria "Or sai chi l'onore / rapire a me volse" ["Now you know / Who wanted to strip me of my honor"] (Andante in D major), in which, now that the culprit is identified, she once again demands vengeance. The vehement opening material yields briefly to the feeling of shock evoked by the memory of her murdered father, but her implacable outbursts return for the exhortation "Vendetta ti chieggio; / la chiede il tuo cuor" ["I ask vengeance of you / As does your heart."], echoed by the basses in canon. From the solemn cadence in D major immediately opens the second part, the excited evocation of the wound and the blood,[7] which leads logically to the repetition of the entire first part; a final cadence is avoided, however, and with another brief reference to the wound and the blood the solemn demand for vengeance is repeated and amplified in a virtuoso stretta.[8]

Donna Anna exits. Don Ottavio remains (scene xiv) to state in recitative that even though it seems inconceivable that a nobleman would be capable "of so black a deed," he will do all he can to give her peace of mind: "I want to disabuse her, or avenge her." At this point, the aria added for the Viennese production of 1788, "Dalla sua pace," is usually performed. This is one of the most often discussed pieces in the opera because of its placidity, which stands in such sharp contrast to the tempestuous sentiments that agitate Donna Anna. There is no doubt that the aria corresponds to the way in which Mozart and Da Ponte viewed the character and in general to the way in which he was traditionally viewed going back to Tirso: a gentle soul. In the opera, he comes to life only in his devotion to Donna Anna (he has his best moment in the vengeance duet of scene iii) and even his aria in Act II paints the same picture.

There is insufficient evidence either in the libretto or the score
that he was depicted this way out of malice, that they wanted to
make him seem ridiculous in his excessive candor, or draw a pointed contrast between his gentility as a *grand seigneur bonhomme* and
the protagonist *grand seigneur méchant homme*, on the one hand,
and the comic, but full-blooded jealousy of Masetto, on the other
hand. To the contrary, Mozart seems to have been grateful to the
tenor Don Ottavio for the services he rendered in the ensembles
and repaid him with arias that, taken out of their dramatic context,
are remarkably beautiful. The Act I aria is perhaps the more beautiful of the two; it follows the text with great subtlety, if to be sure
with moderation and gentility: it even exaggerates his reflected
anger among sighs and tears in the middle section ("S'ella sospira,
/ sospiro anch'io; / è mia quell'ira, / quel pianto è mio" ["If she
sighs, / That sigh is mine; / Mine is that anger; / That tear is
mine"]); it returns with a most delicate harmonic turn to take up
the opening phrase and in amplifying it as usual with a final coda
has still more harmonic surprises in store for the closing line:
"Quel che le incresce / morte mi dà" ["What displeases her / Kills
me"].

For scene xv, Da Ponte, a little mechanically, has Don Ottavio
exit and Leporello immediately enter. Having just said in recitative
that he wants "to abandon this madman forever," he sees him
appear more high-spirited than ever: "Oh Leporello, everything
is going well!" Leporello is not in agreement: "My dear Don
Giovannino, everything is going badly!"[9] He took all the peasants
to the castle and got them half drunk, but Donna Elvira also came
by with Zerlina to say about Don Giovanni "every awful thing that
came to mind"; he neutralized her by showing her outside with the
greatest of courtesy. Don Giovanni approves and, almost tasting
the pleasure he will experience with the peasant girl, sings the so-
called champagne aria, "Fin ch'han dal vino" (Presto in B-flat

major),[10] an aria that has occasioned a great deal of comment. Several commentators have claimed that the character's single true aria should provide the key to his personality; but it is unclear why a character's psychology should be expressed synthetically in a single aria and not also in the recitatives, duets and ensembles, which in fact have already shown various aspects: violence, cynicism, arrogance, unscrupulous dissimulation. There are also claims that Don Giovanni cuts a poor figure as a seducer because in the course of the opera all his attempted conquests prove unsuccessful; but with Zerlina, if the promise was not fulfilled, the caress of the voices was real, as were the intensity of desire and the magnetism of his persuasive sensuality. In this aria, Mozart now shows us the vitality, the unbridled will to enjoy himself without thinking of tomorrow that marks the "young, extremely licentious cavalier," as he is described in the libretto.[11] The joy of living, of recognizing no obstacles to his own desires (and also his sensuality, in the brief minor coloring), are expressed through the forceful rhythm and the overwhelming clarity of the harmony.[12] If one can make one point about this aria it is that its melodies are more instrumental than vocal; it demands a precision and a brilliance that few voices can achieve, and the least slowing down renders it banal.

5. Act I, Scenes xvi-xix

The scene changes. In Don Giovanni's garden, with the palace windows illuminated (therefore the evening of the second day has already arrived), Zerlina tries to appease Masetto; she claims she is innocent, that the cavalier "did not even touch the tip of [her] finger."[13] She meekly offers herself up to his blows (since Masetto wants to make peace) singing the aria "Batti, batti, o bel Masetto" (Andante grazioso in F major), the first part of which, in 2/4, corresponding to the first two quatrains of the text, is in itself already completely developed, caressing and insinuating. Mozart adds to this another verse with a veiled hint of triumph: "Ah, lo vedo, non hai core" ["Ah, I see you do not have the heart to do this"], leading to a cadence that serves as only a momentary pause: with a wonderful intervallic inversion it blossoms into the close of the aria in 6/8, which seals her success: "Pace, pace, o mio tesoro."[14] Masetto is won over, but Don Giovanni's voice is heard from inside the palace, and Zerlina's uneasiness arouses new suspicions. Thus the finale to Act I begins with the duet "Presto, presto . . . pria ch'ei venga" (Allegro in C major); Masetto wants to hide so that he can spy upon Zerlina's meeting with Don Giovanni. Zerlina tries in vain to dissuade him: she fears for him but also begins to fear the spell that Don Giovanni wields over her. The sound of the brass announces the arrival of Don Giovanni and his servants (scene xvii) to wake up the peasants, who have been asleep in the garden up to this point, and to invite them into the palace "to the ballroom." The chorus goes off, and the Allegro ends with a diminuendo; Zerlina sings an anxious and bewildered phrase ("Tra questi alberi celata / si può dar che non mi veda" ["Hidden amidst these trees / perhaps he won't see me"]. (Andante in 3/4). Don Giovanni captures her in flight and repeats her phrase with an air of satisfaction. He joins her and, despite her pleas, begins to envelop her in his charm. However, he adopts another approach upon seeing Masetto (modulation to d minor); he pulls him out from his hiding place and assumes toward both of them a tone of condescending protectiveness (modulation to C major). In the end, all three enter the palace in apparent accord, accompanied by the sounds coming from a small orchestra inside (clarinets, horns, and strings). After four transitional measures, the orchestra begins an Allegretto with new figures for the entrance of the three maskers (scene xvi-ii): they are Donna Elvira who incites this action, Don Ottavio who reassures himself by reassuring Donna Anna, and Donna Anna who is more hesitant than the others ("temo pel caro sposo / e per noi temo ancor" ["I fear for my dear fiancé / And I fear for us also"]). When a window onto the garden opens, music from inside is heard once more (this time it is the minuet in F major); Leporello and Don Giovanni espy the masked figures and invite them in (scene xix); they close the window and the music to the minuet ceases. The three pause for a moment to collect themselves in prayer (Adagio); the fervent opening phrase of Donna Anna and Don Ottavio, "Protegga il giusto cielo / lo zelo del mio cor," characterizes this passage as a prayer most beautiful in its unusual musical expression; their voices are then interwoven with Donna Elvira's (who asks heaven for vengeance) in a daring counterpoint of sophisticated virtuoso figuration, from which emerges more than the feelings of each individual their common need to embrace each other before confronting the risk that awaits them.

6. Act I, Scenes xx-xxi

The score indicates a brief pause after the trio of the maskers, and the cadence on B-flat prepares the beginning of the next piece in E-flat; but there may have been a longer interval in performance because a change of scene transfers the action inside the palace. The Allegro in 6/8, the rhythm of the country dance of scene vii (now more agitated because of the latent tensions in the charac-ters), provides a background that soon fills out into a quartet: Don Giovanni and Leporello invite the groups of dancers to rest;

Masetto and Zerlina are apprehensive ("Troppo dolce comincia la scena; / in amaro potria terminar" ["The scene begins too sweetly; / It may well end bitterly"]); Don Giovanni flatters Zerlina, and Leporello imitates him with other girls, but all three, Zerlina included, keep an eye on Masetto. The entrance of the three maskers welcomed by Leporello (scene xxi) provides a diversion (Maestoso in C major); the exchange of ceremony between the trio and Don Giovanni is unexpectedly amplified by a chorus (as was noted above) on the host's final words: "Viva la libertà!" Then the festivities begin again. On Don Giovanni's orders, the first of the three orchestras onstage (oboes, horns, and strings) begins playing the minuet once again (now in G major), which from this point onward provides the pompous and mannered facade behind which the intrigue will rapidly unfold. Leporello arranges the couples for the dance and tries to make Masetto dance also, though the latter resists; the trio of maskers looks on suspiciously; Don Giovanni, who from the start has been pressuring Zerlina to dance with him, finally succeeds when, in the course of the minuet, the second orchestra (of violins and double basses) starts a contredanse. With celebrated virtuosity Mozart superimposes over the first two a third orchestra (also of violins and double basses), which plays a popular type of waltz (a *teitsch*), which Leporello finally succeeds in making Masetto dance.[15] In the course of dancing, Don Giovanni succeeds in carrying Zerlina off; but he has been observed by many people, and the girl's loud scream from inside brings the stage music to a halt; at this point the main orchestra resumes (Allegro assai) with a crescendo and rapid modulations (E-flat, b-flat minor, c minor, d minor), while from inside Zerlina continues to scream for help, and onstage they try to force the door open. This proves to be unnecessary: Don Giovanni bursts onto the stage (Andante maestoso in F major) dragging Leporello and threatening him with his sword: "Ecco il birbo che l'ha offesa!" ["Here is the rascal who offended her"]. But no one believes him: Don Ottavio "takes out a pistol" and the trio of maskers in canonic entries unmask themselves ("L'empio crede con tal frode / di nasconder l'empietà" ["The wicked man believes that with this deception / He can hide his wickedness"]); Masetto and Zerlina join them in a concerted ensemble ("Tutto, tutto già si sa" ["All is known."]) and the agitated final Allegro in C major is unleashed; it pits Don Giovanni and Leporello against the five other characters and the chorus. The finale approaches a climax through increasingly urgent rhythms and threats, such as "un tuon della vendetta" ["the thundering of vengeance"] with lightning not far behind. Don Giovanni reacts proudly after a brief moment of uncertainty: "ma non manca in me il coraggio: / non mi perdo o mi confondo. / Se cadesse ancora il mondo / nulla mai temer mi fa!" ["But I do not lack courage. / I will not lose my head. / Even if the world should fall, / Nothing would make me fear"] The threatening paroxysm can only lead to the end of the act leaving to the audience's imagination how such a tense situation could resolve itself. Theatrical conventions permit, nay demand, that the lightning bolt remain suspended.

7. Act II, Scenes i-vi

At the beginning of Act II, Don Giovanni seems to have completely forgotten the impending threat. It is still night, though it is not clear of what day,[16] and he is already in the street with Leporello near the house where Donna Elvira is lodging; together they sing a typically comic duet, "Eh, via buffone, non mi seccar" (Allegro assai in G major), each taking up the other's themes even though they are in disagreement. In the recitative that follows,

Don Giovanni has even more convincing arguments to keep Leporello from leaving him: he gives him money but rejects the suggestion of leaving the ladies alone: "Lasciar le donne? Sai ch'elle per me / son necessarie più che il pan che mangio, / più che l'aria che spiro!" ["Leave the ladies alone? You know / That I need them more than I need the bread that I eat, / More than the air that I breathe!"] He has already eyed Donna Elvira's maid,[17] and to have greater probability of success asks and obtains from Leporello an exchange of garments. Scene ii begins when Donna Elvira comes to the balcony and sings the opening passage of the trio (Andante in A major), "Ah, taci, ingiusto core . . . / è colpa aver pietà" ["Ah, silence, unjust heart . . . / It is wrong to feel pity"]; whose close is prolonged with a creeping figure of the basses above which the two men plot. After a single transitional measure, the entire period is repeated in E major, and in this key Don Giovanni invokes "Elvira, idolo mio!" and repeats the melody, parodying it; he grows more fervent, however, and his melody becomes persuasive (subtle melodic and harmonic variants transfigure it) and intensifies the passionate emphasis even more with a modulation to C major (the phrase "Discendi, o gioia bella" ["Descend, o fair jewel"] shamelessly anticipates the opening phrase of the serenade that he will sing to her maid in the following scene). The entire trio (it is impossible to continue to analyze it) is a masterpiece of balance between passion and parody, emphasis and irony, seduction and cynicism ("che bel colpetto è questo!" ["What a coup this is!"]). Elvira retires from the balcony to go down to meet Don Giovanni, but the latter in high spirits has another surprise in store: he wants Leporello to meet her pretending to be him and take her off; the means of persuasion this time is the threat of a pistol. Elvira exits the house (scene iii); Leporello is clumsy and ill at ease, but she does not perceive the deception. Don Giovanni, to one side, simulates the sound of a duel to make them flee; he

succeeds and sings to the accompaniment of a mandolin and violins the serenade "Deh, vieni alla finestra" (Allegretto in D major),
two strophes in apparently popular style, but made precious by a
delicate harmonic turn and above all charged with the magic of
seduction this character is capable of.

Don Giovanni looks toward the window (scene iv), but the
servant of his desires, like Tirso's Donna Anna never appears
onstage. What prevents this is a consequence of something that
happened in Act I: Masetto and a number of peasants have armed
themselves and gone in search of Don Giovanni to avenge themselves. Thanks to the exchange of clothes, Don Giovanni can
pretend to be Leporello (a most skillful invention of Da Ponte's),
and by pretending he wants to avenge himself against his master
he succeeds in placing himself at the head of this enterprise; he
gives orders singing a comic aria that is both spirited and subtle:
"Metà di voi qua vadano, / e gli altri vadan là, / e pian pianin lo
cerchino: / lontan non fia di qua." ["Half of you go this way, / And
half of you go that way, / And very slowly search for him: / He
won't be far from here"]. Cynically he describes the clothes that he
gave Leporello and the hat "with white feathers"; and he does not
hesitate to say "Strike him, wound him: / That will be my master."
But to Masetto he says, "You alone will come with me" and
promises that together they will do "what else had to be done, and
presently [Masetto] will see what that is." Left alone (scene v),
Don Giovanni has Masetto give him his weapons so that he can
examine them and when he has him defenseless and in his power
he beats him furiously and leaves him there in pain. Toward his
cries, Zerlina runs carrying a lamp (scene vi); she recognizes her
man and listens to the list of injuries inflicted upon him—he
says—by Leporello "or some devil who looks like him." He asks
her to take him home where he should have been if he had not
been led astray by "mad jealousy" (we must not forget that this is

their wedding night). But first, she naturally sings an aria: "Vedrai, carino, / se sei buonino, che bel rimedio / ti voglio dar" ["You will see, my dear, / If you are a good little boy, what a fine remedy / I will give you"] (Grazioso in C major), whose opening melody resembles the first aria of Gazzaniga's Donna Elvira. But Gazzaniga's aria expressed a deluded and defeated woman; Mozart's aria, a bit protectively consoling, and a bit maliciously provoking, expresses more subtly the triumphant resources of apparent fragility.

8. Act II, Scenes vii-xi

Leporello and Donna Elvira come upon, we know not how, a "dark courtyard in Donna Anna's house" (scene vii). Leporello continues to pretend to be Don Giovanni, but he now wants to rid himself of her company. He goes off in the dark, and she sings, preceded by uncertain harmonies in a phrase that expresses discouragement, "Sola, sola, in buio loco / palpitar il cor mi sento" ["All alone in this dark place / I feel my heart beating"] (Andante in B-flat). This is the beginning of the celebrated sextet, which encompasses the events and states of being of three successive scenes of the libretto. While clumsily attempting to find a way out, Leporello responds to Elvira's phrase from another corner (but she does not hear him). A striking modulation from B flat to D major and the addition of trumpets and timpani brighten the sound of the orchestra: this represents the light that accompanies the entrance of Donna Anna and Don Ottavio followed by servants with burning torches. Upon Ottavio's broad phrase, "Tergi il ciglio, o vita mia" ["Dry your tears, o my life"] in D major, the orchestra begins a symphonic development that continues with Donna Anna's response, "Lascia almeno alla mia pena / questo piccolo ristoro" ["Grant this small relief / at least to my pain"], with a series of rapid modulations (d minor, B-flat, c minor, e-flat minor, c minor, f minor, d-flat minor, c minor) supporting a supple, sorrowful melodic line ("sol la morte, o mio tesoro, / il mio pianto può finir" ["Death alone, my treasure, / Will end my tears"]). The attention then turns toward Elvira, who expresses her discomfort, even more than in her voice, in a chromatically descending line of the violins with an almost sobbing rhythm, and Leporello, whose comic realism is depicted in the adherence of his singing to typical bass cadential formulas. When he has finally found the exit, his way is blocked by Zerlina and Masetto (who have not yet made their way home) (scene viii); Donna Anna and Don Ottavio also see him, and everyone mistakes him for Don Giovanni; they attack him: "Ah, mora il perfido / che m'ha tradito!" [Ah, let the perfidious one who betrayed me die!"] Donna Elvira comes forward to protect him (once again she is accompanied by the descending figure in the violins): "È mio marito, / pietà, pietà!" ["He is my husband, / Have pity!"] and for an instant imposes her descending chromaticism on her persecutors who are none too sure of themselves (either because of meekness or fear) even though they twice state with comic fury "No, no: morrà!" ["No, he will die!"] Finally, Leporello reveals himself, pathetically asking for mercy (in g minor), and the others, including Donna Elvira, express surprise and mistrust with harmonies that rise by half steps from the dominant on g minor to c minor, and remain on c minor with a question that goes unanswered. After a brief pause, the Allegro molto begins in the E-flat of the sextet proper: Leporello begins with two phrases of equal length in unison with the bass: "Mille torbidi pensieri / mi s'aggiran per la testa" ["A thousand troubled thoughts / Are whirling about my head"], to each of which the other five respond softly in chorus. Then their thoughts diverge, although they continue to alternate: Leporello in the rapid patter of comic basses, thinks how he can save himself in this situation ("Se mi salvo in tal periglio / è un prodigio in verità" ["If I save myself from this danger, / It will truly be a miracle"]), while the others have not yet recovered from the surprise and dramatize their amazement ("Che giornata, o stelle, è questa! / Che impensata novità!" ["Oh stars, what a day this has been! / What unimagined events!"]). But all that agitates the characters has already been said, and the piece continues purely for the sake of musical development, nevertheless not lacking in further musical motives of interest; twice, on an unexpected D-flat chord, Donna Anna lets loose above the others a rapid coloratura passage; and when the closing cadence appears near, a sudden piano that leaves the voices almost deprived of instrumental support postpones the closing stretta. With the final measures of the closing ritornello, Donna Anna exits.

If, in accordance with Dent's hypothesis, the sextet was originally intended as the close of an act (Act III of four acts), we would have had another example of an effective operatic finale that leaves to the audience's imagination how the various characters would be able to resume their activities after experiencing such a climactic paroxysm. With the action divided into only two acts, Da Ponte had to resolve this problem. Donna Anna exits because she has nothing against Leporello; but all the others want to punish him (scene ix): Zerlina for the mistreatment she believes he inflicted upon Masetto; Donna Elvira because he substituted for Don Giovanni; Don Ottavio because he suspects him of dark intrigue. His defense is the aria "Ah, pietà, signori miei" (Allegro assai in G major), clever in the choice of the central argument ("del padron la prepotenza / l'innocenza mi rubò" ["My master's power over me / Robbed me of my innocence"]), the attenuating circumstances with regard to Donna Elvira, and the alibi with regard to Zerlina and Masetto (he was with Donna Elvira). He does not know how to respond to Don Ottavio, but in his apparent confusion he has found the exit and now flees; Mozart depicts his flight in a characteristic manner with a diminuendo in the measures of the closing ritornello.

It is useless to pursue him, and Don Ottavio returns to the more important problem (scene x): he offers everyone hospitality and . . . vengeance: "un ricorso / vo' a fare a chi si deve, e in pochi istanti / vendicarvi prometto. / Così vuole dover, pietade, affetto" ["I must appeal / To the authorities and in a little while / I promise to avenge you. / This, duty, pity and affection demand"]. Affection is not the last thing on his mind: he tenderly commends Donna Anna to his new friends (who would probably never have entered his life were it not for the confusion caused by Don Giovanni); and he does this in a long aria, "Il mio tesoro intanto / andate a consolar" (Andante in B-flat major), which begins softly with muted violins, gives way in the second part to duty ("Ditele che i suoi torti / io vado a vendicare" ["Tell her that I go / To avenge her wrongs"]) and extinguishes the tenuous expressions of avenging "death and destruction" in an extended and graceful coloratura that returns to the meek tenderness of the opening theme. There would have been no reason for this aria, if the sextet had actually functioned as an act finale; it was, however, cut in the Viennese production[18] and replaced by an absurdly comic episode that is usually omitted today—three added scenes that hook up to the end of Leporello's aria in scene ix.[19] The Viennese addition to scene xi, however, music that was added for the singer Caterina Cavalieri, has remained part of the performance tradition of the opera: Donna Elvira remains alone in the courtyard of Donna Anna's house, which is no longer dark, to sing a fine recitative, accompanied at first with vehement punctuations by the strings

(Allegro assai) and later in a more intimate and moving manner. The thought of Don Giovanni's fate troubles her: she is already experiencing the conflicting emotions that later will lead her to his house to deliver a final desperate admonition; she asks herself "Perché questi sospiri e queste ambasce?" ["Why these sighs and why this distress?"] The answer, less effective than the question, is in the aria that follows, a delicately orchestrated rondo (Allegretto in E flat), in which the main theme (to the words "Mi tradì quell'alma ingrata! / infelice, oddio! mi fa!" ["That ungrateful soul betrayed me! / Oh God, he made me miserable!"]) should express resentment, and the various episodes that alternate with it, rich in orchestral figures, pity. But the aria is above all what in that time would have been called an *aria di mezzo carattere*, written by Mozart to please a singer whom he held in high esteem and to permit her to display her graceful legato style.[20] The concession was all the more necessary because Donna Anna already had the same type of aria, also a rondo (as we shall see in scene xiii).

9. Act II, Scenes xii-xiv

At this point, Da Ponte's libretto shows signs of haste in that the action changes place three times in a row with the beginning of each new scene (scene xiv is a brief appendix to scene xiii). Scene xii takes place by moonlight in a graveyard with various equestrian monuments including the Commendatore's.[21] Don Giovanni enters by scaling the wall, happy to have eluded someone in pursuit of him. To Leporello, who arrives shortly afterward, he narrates with derisive laughter the good fortune he enjoyed with a "delicately beautiful young" girl who mistook him for Leporello.[22]

Suddenly from among the tombs a stern voice accompanied by chords played by three trombones (along with oboes, clarinets, bassoons, cellos, and double basses) admonishes him: "Di rider finirai pria dell'aurora" ["You will stop laughing by dawn"], and renews the admonishment when Don Giovanni "places his hand on his sword and searches here and there in the graveyard striking various statues": "Ribaldo audace! / lascia a' morti la pace!" ["Audacious rascal! / Leave the dead in peace!"] Today the mysterious voice no longer has the same effect as it did then when the use of trombones was rare in opera,[23] but even Mozart does not seem to have given them particular weight. They serve above all to create the paroxysm of fear in Leporello and to prepare the comic duet "O statua gentilissima" (Allegro in E major) (but first there is the reading of the inscription). In the duet, Leporello struggles between his own superstitious fear and the sadistic stubbornness of his master who threatens him and forces him to speak to the statue and invite him to dinner; the solemn rhetoric with which he addresses the statue is comic, as are the leaps of a descending seventh that interrupt the invitation each time his courage fails him, and also comic are the screams of dismay when the phrase is finally finished: "Ah, ah, che scena è questa! / oh ciel, chinò la testa!" ["Ah, what a scene this is! / Oh heaven, he nodded his head!"] The comedy also reflects upon the statue whose nod Leporello imitates with the inflections of his own voice; the only moment that is free of comedy is the moment of astonishment on Don Giovanni's part when the statue laconically and without trombones accepts his invitation.[24] The close, in which master and servant decide to go home, depicts the characters on their way and once more reflects their departure through an orchestral diminuendo.

Scene xiii (it is a new day and we are in Donna Anna's house) troubles most commentators.[25] One must admit that its fine musical points, valid in the immediate context, do not constitute positive elements in the opera as a whole; but I have already noted that this scene belongs to a section of the libretto that was unable to achieve a more orderly arrangement. It should be noted further that it is part of the design of Act II to balance the brutality and egoism of purely physical love, expressed through Don Giovanni, with the incarnation of more altruistic love, expressed through Zerlina in scene vi, Don Ottavio in scene x, Donna Elvira in scene x (to which can then be added scene xi), and finally through Donna Anna, who here is divided between her love for Don Ottavio, on the one hand, and, on the other, her sorrow for the death of her father and the respect due his memory.[26] To Don Otaovio's new proposal for an immediate wedding she responds with the recitative "Crudele? Ah no, mio bene!" (first Risoluto, then Larghetto, which anticipates the string figure of the aria) and then with the aria "Non mi dir, bell'idol mio." Its first part (Larghetto in F major) is a rondo (the designation is Mozart's own)[27] and is intended, like Donna Elvira's rondo in scene xi, to show the ability of the singer in the legato and *affettuoso* style (excellent also are the orchestral themes at the points where the orchestra stands out from the vocal part). The second part (Allegretto moderato) begins with a theme that is similarly *affettuoso* and legato, but it then expands, postponing the close, in an elaborate display of virtuosity. A few measures of recitative for Don Ottavio constitute scene xiv, but they add nothing new.

10. Act II, Scenes xv-xvii

A final change of scene carries us to Don Giovanni's palace. This coincides with the beginning of the finale, in which the first piece

(Allegro vivace) is in D major, the key of the overture and the close of the opera, whether it ends with scene xvii or the epilogue that follows.[28] The orchestra begins by presenting the two themes that will serve Don Giovanni immediately afterward, the assertive fanfare stated twice, for "Già la mensa è preparata" ["The meal is already prepared"] and (directed toward the players) "Voi sonate, amici cari" ["Play, dear friends"], and the scale ascent above a tonic pedal of "giacché spendo i miei danari, / io mi voglio divertir" ["Since I'm spending my money, / I want to enjoy myself"]. Leporello is "most ready to serve," and the consumption of the first course coincides with the dinner music of the stage orchestra, which plays three pieces in succession that were well known to the audiences of the time.[29] Leporello immediately recognizes the first (he says: "Bravi! Cosa rara!"), a piece from the finale to Act I of *Una cosa rara* by Martin y Soler (Allegretto in D major); he also recognizes the second ("Evvivano *I litiganti!*"), the aria "Come un agnello" from *I pretendenti delusi* by Giuseppe Sarti.[30] At the third, he says, without naming the work, "This one I know only too well"; it is the aria "Non più andrai, farfallone amoroso" from *Le nozze di Figaro* (Act I, scene viii), one of the arias that enjoyed the greatest success in Prague the preceding February. Dinner proceeds during the three pieces with Leporello, who after the "crazy night" he has experienced is almost faint with hunger, gazing enviously at the "giant mouthfuls" consumed by his master, and Don Giovanni as always taking pleasure in torturing him. On the final chord of the stage orchestra's third piece, Donna Elvira bursts into the room (scene xvi). In a series of brief phrases (Allegro assai in 3/4) played by the full orchestra with chords alternating between forte and piano, she addresses Don Giovanni excitedly: "L'ultima prova / dell'amor mio / ancor vogl'io / fare con te. / Più non rammento / gl'inganni tuoi: / pietade io sento" ["The last proof / Of my love / I still want / To show you. / I no longer remember /

Your deceptions: / I feel pity"] To entreat him she kneels before him; even Leporello is shaken, but Don Giovanni, who kneels also with affected courtesy, is all derision. At her insistence that he "change his way of living," he responds disdainfully: "Lascia ch'io mangi / e, se ti piace, / mangia con me" ["Let me eat, / And if you like, / Join me"]. This is too much: the dialogue grows into a trio, from which emerges every now and then Don Giovanni's depraved line: "Vivan le femmine! / Viva il buon vino! / sostegno e gloria / d'umanità" ["Long live women! / Long live wine! / Sustenance and glory / of humanity!"], which uses an assertive theme from the orchestra. Leporello is indignant and touched at the same time, but Donna Elvira's curses are more cutting: "Restati, barbaro, / nel lezzo immondo, / esempio orribile / d'iniquità" ["Wallow, barbarian, / In your stinking filth, / A horrible example / Of wickedness!"]

She exits the door accompanied by an orchestral crescendo but immediately returns with a scream and flees by the other door.[31] Leporello goes to investigate and also lets out a scream, which Don Giovanni describes as "possessed." The dramatic tension is intensified, yet there is still time for an episode that could appear comic, but that Mozart succeeds in rendering with a degree of realism that does not clash with what precedes it and what will follow. After an orchestral pause on a chord that would make one predict a resolution to D major, Leporello begins in F major, pianissimo, the narration of what he has seen (Allegro molto in 4/4): "d'uom . . . di . . . sasso . . . l'uomo bianco . . ." ["the man of stone, the pale-faced man"], which goes "ta, ta, ta, ta" (unison from the full orchestra). At this point, one hears knocking at the door, and Don Giovanni decides to go to open it himself, while Leporello ends his story, again under his breath (and in F major), crouching under the table. The pivot chord of a minor in first inversion on which Don Giovanni resolutely opens the door is immediately overwhelmed (scene xvii) by a fortissimo from the entire orchestra reinforced by the clangor of trumpets and trombones. Two drawn-out dissonant chords,[32] during which the immobile figure of the statue appears in the door frame; then the piano chords of the strings begin to accompany the cold and inflexible voice of the Commendatore (Andante in d minor) with a trochaic rhythm that reflects the inevitability of what is about to take place more than it depicts the majestic stride of the supernatural apparition. The themes already heard in the slow introduction to the overture are restated and coordinated with a rapid succession of varying emotions:[33] the syncopated figure of the violins with which Don Giovanni expresses surprise mixed with anxiety (an emotion not expressed in his words); the insistently cadencing sforzati in g minor with which he regains his composure more to conform to his own self-image than to honor his unexpected guest; and the tortuous descending figure with which Leporello expresses reluctance and fear. The Commendatore's voice expresses through unusual melodic intervals that his condition transcends that of mortals ("Non si pasce di cibo mortale / chi si pasce di cibo celeste" ["He who eats heavenly food / Does not eat earthly food"]);[34] and then turns to the lean, passionless linearity that marks him throughout the scene. Passionless is the character, engaged in fulfilling the will of a higher power, but the opposite is true of both his interlocutors and the audience, in whom Mozart creates dramatic resonances by superimposing unexpected harmonies above the rigidity of the voices. While the trochaic figure continues as a rhythmic ostinato in the basses and timpani, the harmonies and the ascending and descending scales of the violins and flutes begin to change the color of the implacable declamation fixed on the pedal point A. Whatever comic intention Da Ponte may have had in Leporello's words ("La terzana d'aver mi sembra / e le membra fermar più non so" ["I seem to have a fever / And I've lost control of my limbs"]), the character has lost all his vitality and is reduced to providing rhythmic and harmonic support to the forced arrogance of Don Giovanni's replies. The Commendatore's voice is employed in a slow ascent by half steps to return the invitation to dinner, in accordance with tradition; Don Giovanni responds above the syncopated motive of the violins (now in b-flat minor), revealing one of his basic character traits: "A torto di viltate / tacciato mai sarò!" ["With the charge of cowardice / May I never be stained!"] The inhuman voice follows him closely with an inhuman drawing out of melodic intervals: "Risolvi . . . Verrai?" ["Decide . . . Will you come?"][35] Don Giovanni ennobles himself with the proud chivalry of his reply: "Ho fermo il core in petto, / non ho timor: verrò!" ["The heart in my breast is firm. / I do not fear: I will come."], and offers, as he has just been requested to, his hand as pledge of his promise. On a diminished seventh chord and string tremolos, the tempo grows faster and the basses (as in the duel scene) enrich with rapid scales a new version of the trochaic rhythm falling precipitously upon Don Giovanni's last two refusals to the insistent demands to repent. The Commendatore's final phrase (for he then disappears), "Ah! tempo più non v'è!" ["Ah, there is no more time!"], once more draws upon unusual intervals sung pianissimo in unison with the trombones and with string tremolo;[36] this gives way to an even faster tempo, to the descending flickers of the strings, to the rapidly modulating harmonies of the infernal scene, for which a backstage chorus of spectral voices (basses in unison) sing. Don Giovanni's exclamations are tragic, tormented and raving; but no less tragic is their reflection in Leporello's words: "Che ceffo disperato! . . . / che gesti da dannato! . . . / che gridi! che lamenti! . . . / come mi fa terror!" ["Such signs of desperation! / The gestures of the damned! / What shouts! What laments! How they terrify me!"]; then Don Giovanni sinks, and a diminuendo no less rapid than the rest of the scene leads to the closing D-major chords (the key of the overture).

11. Act II, Scene the Last, Epilogue

The "final scene" is an epilogue in the narrowest sense of the word, to the extent that the Viennese production of 1788 was able to omit it (a temptation that more recent productions have also fallen prey to). In its stead, in the libretto for that production, the characters all return to the stage at the moment Don Giovanni sinks down, "gaze about, scream, flee, and the curtain falls"; leaving once again to the audience's imagination what happens to the characters of an opera after the closing chord of the finale that finds them all onstage. With regard to *Don Giovanni*, several considerations opposed this view of operatic finales. Inherent in the theme was the tradition that after the death of the protagonist at least some of the characters should draw the necessary exemplary conclusions and together attempt to place their lives in order once again after such confusion. It would never even have been considered to have an opera, especially a comic opera, end on a tragic note. I do not doubt that *Don Giovanni* was conceived as a comic opera, not only because of the label *dramma giocoso* given it by its authors and the many elements of comedy that it contains, but also because all the most intensely dramatic and moving material in it would have been more difficult to realize without the expressive possibilities and flexible structure that the tradition of comic opera provided Mozart. For me therefore the epilogue is an essential part of the opera and in examining it as such I will seize the opportunity it presents to review together with Mozart all the characters, those present onstage and those who, while no longer there, weigh heavily on everyone's memory.

It is of no use to ask why earthly justice, pursued by Don Ottavio, awaited an improbable hour of the night to go into action; nor how not only Don Ottavio and Donna Anna, but also Donna Elvira, Zerlina, and Masetto have come together with the "ministers of justice" to burst into Don Giovanni's home. Ready for action, without any prelude other than two measures of orchestral introduction (Allegro assai in 3/4, G major) four of them declare their wish to vent their fury on the "perfidious, unworthy one"; the fifth, Donna Anna, is too much a lady to propose such direct action, but she echoes them by saying: "Solo mirandolo / stretto in catene / alle mie pene / calma darò" ["Only when I see him / Clasped in chains / Will my pain / Be assuaged"] Leporello, still utterly confused, disabuses them; he narrates what has happened in pure comic style, with disconnected phrases, from which only emerges that "Venne un colosso . . ." and that "Giusto là sotto / diede il gran botto, / giusto là il diavolo / s'el trangugiò" ["A colossus appeared. / . . . Down there / Dealt the great blow. / There the devil / Gulped him down"]. This is enough, however, to cut short further questions and provides the opportunity for Donna Elvira to provide some confirmation, "Ah certo è l'ombra / che m'incontrò" ["Ah, surely that was the shade / That I met"]; however mechanical and absurd the repetition by the others ("Ah, certo è l'ombra / che l'incontrò!"), Mozart uses it to have all the characters experience, better than through Leporello's narration, a shiver, as a consequence of the mysterious event that has just occurred. The Allegro assai ends after a soft chromatic descent with all the voices on a sustained dominant chord, which stands suspended, like a question: and now? . . .

The first to answer, as befits his noble rank, is Don Ottavio, who turns to Donna Anna to insist in his best singing style on an immediate wedding (Larghetto in G major). And with just as much tenderness, indeed taking up his phrase almost unaltered, she asks him to wait "another year," and they join in a tender duet that alternates and interweaves the voices on the words "Al desio di chi t'adora [m'adora, for Don Ottavio] / ceder deve un fido amor." ["To the wishes of someone who loves you / A faithful lover must accede"]. This postponement, like all Donna Anna's earlier refusals, is also taken as evidence of the theory that she was deeply affected, perhaps without realizing it, by the erotic ardor of Don Giovanni, and that she can no longer tolerate Don Ottavio's sentimental effusions; all the more so since not even the most indulgent of commentators are sparing of accusations of ineptitude and even suspicions of lack of virility with regard to Don Ottavio. These are slanders, for Don Ottavio plays the part of the *primo innamorato* conforming to a long tradition, with no less dignity and virility than any other tenor in a similar role—it suffices to mention Belmonte's three arias in *Die Entführung aus dem Serail* and the aria Gazzaniga gives to his tenor Don Giovanni. That Mozart could overcome the limits of this convention is shown by the warmth that loving affection acquires in his baritone Don Giovanni; but to do the same for the less important character of Don Ottavio would have rendered the figure of the protagonist less effective. As for Donna Anna, if we want to observe her in the moment—after she faints in Act I, scene iii—in which she has least control over herself, when her words may be most revealing, even then she refers to her unknown assailant not as the man who offended her but as her father's murderer. Toward Ottavio she always expresses loving concern: at a moment they are both at risk, she thinks of him before herself ("Temo pel caro sposo / e per noi temo ancor," Act I, scene xix). And even Mozart, here in the epilogue as already in the aria "Non mi dir, bell'idol mio," shows clearly she is in love with her fiancé. Refusals and postponements are therefore justified by her intense sorrow over the death of her father (which Mozart expresses most beautifully, for example, in the brief duet inserted into the Act II sextet), and the key to her character is her intense filial love and her exaggerated concept of the familial and societal regard due his memory.[37] From this derives the violence with which she demands vengeance in Act I, in an exceptional situation in which Mozart was able to extract from his fantasy incredible expressions of force and novelty. For this reason, she has been exalted unanimously as an implacable figure of revenge, as she appears in Act I; or also as a possible instrument for the redemption of Don Giovanni's soul, in any case as his female antagonist; and the different expressions that she assumes in Act II have been viewed with embarrassment or even disgust.[38]

With regard to Donna Anna, a lady of the highest social station, we know something of her state of mind and above all her firm and determined will; nothing more. Donna Elvira may also be noble (her deportment impresses Donna Anna and Don Ottavio in Act I, scene xi), but she does not share the same social station, considering that she travels alone in search of Don Giovanni without the support of friends or family. The text and music characterize her from her very first appearance with emphatic expressions. With regard to her language, Leporello's remark "Pare un libro stampato" ["She sounds like a printed book"]. also makes note of this; with regard to her music, the many melodic leaps and the tense rhythms of her melodies in Act I speak to this point, in the two arias of scenes v and x, and at the beginning of the quartet "Non ti fidar, o misera." But emphasis is only a shield to protect her vulnerability and generosity. Leporello's catalogue aria reveals to her a reality worse than she had suspected, and she makes it her duty to prevent other victims from falling into the deception that has made her so unhappy. She is the impetus behind the expedition of the three maskers at the festivities in Don Giovanni's palace, and even though in the trio prayer that precedes this she sings "Vendichi il giusto cielo / il mio tradito amor" ["Let just heaven avenge / My betrayed love."] after they have entered she makes sure to point out to her companions the "peasant girl" who is in danger, i.e., Zerlina. When the plot is foiled, in large part because of her, she begins to fear for Don Giovanni and to pity him; this is clear from her balcony soliloquy at the beginning of the protean trio in Act II, scene ii. Love renders her defenseless (and she knows this) before Don Giovanni's new flattery and new promises, which make her embark upon the unlikely and tragi-comic adventure of wandering about with Leporello. She is saved from the ridiculous by the moving expressions Mozart fashions for her in the sextet "Sola, sola, in buio loco," in the recitative of scene xi (added for Vienna) and in part also in the aria of the same scene, "Mi tradì quell'alma ingrata," which is certainly the most impassioned of the three arias Mozart wrote in the legato style for the three female roles. In the end, the suppliant anxiety of her final appeal to Don Giovanni, lean and incisive in her sudden outburst and in her contained shame, is one of the most dramatic moments in the opera, rendered bitter through the protagonist's sarcastic remarks.

In the epilogue, Donna Elvira is the first to speak after the exchanges of tender *fioriture* between Donna Anna and Don Ottavio; she has one brief phrase, "Io men vado in un ritiro / a finir la vita mia" ["I will enter a covent / To finish my life"], which Mozart distinguishes through a sudden modulation (to e minor) from the words of the couple that have already spoken and the couple who will follow with the same phrase except in D major, Zerlina and Masetto; together the two announce "Noi, Masetto [Zerlina], a casa andiamo / a cenar in compagnia" ["We will go home / To dine together"]. The last to speak, Leporello, expresses with his own melody a design at odds with the dreams of greatness embraced in the opening scene of the opera: "Ed io vado all'osteria /

a trovar padron miglior" ["And I will go to the inn / To find a better master"]. Zerlina, Masetto, and Leporello then sing in unison a rather coarse quip: "Resti dunque quel birbon / con Proserpina e Pluton" ["Let the scoundrel abide / with Proserpine and Pluto"] prelude to the final piece and to the moral of the opera, to which I will return after completing our review of the characters.

Zerlina is a comic character, but not at all a secondary figure. Mozart shows a certain partiality toward her by giving her a part that is almost as extensive as that of the other two women, and making it even longer later through the addition of three new scenes for the Viennese production, one of which includes a comic duet. She derives from Goldoni's shepherdess Elisa more than the other peasant girls and fishermaids seduced on the stage by Don Giovanni over the course of two centuries (of course, this was for the most part a matter concerning the librettist Da Ponte). But Elisa, an Arcadian and therefore literary shepherdess, is almost a lady of letters herself, while Zerlina is more authentically close to nature, to be sure a nature seen through the eyes of Da Ponte and Mozart, neither of whom had ever had anything to do with work in the fields. Furthermore, Elisa is viewed by Goldoni with the severe eyes of a moralist, while Zerlina is treated indulgently by a moral but not moralistic human being like Mozart (not to speak of Da Ponte). From this comes a girl like so many in the petit bourgeois world of Salzburg or Vienna, natural in that she knows that men like her and that she likes men. She is sincere in her love for well-built, robust, and stubborn Masetto, whom she knows how to dominate with a little cunning and cajolery; but the fine cavalier also tempts her by giving her exaggerated compliments, speaking so smoothly, and putting so much sweetness into his ardent invitation and so much ardor into the sweetness of his promises. I am not certain that she believes in his promises (in this she is Don

Giovanni's female counterpart); but perhaps she considers surrender a venial sin and hesitates not because the decision seems to her
irreparable but because of her provocative woman's instinct.
Mozart gives us a glimpse of all this with subtle and well-calibrated
inflections in a recitative and duet and renders with the same pen-
etrating insight the fear she experiences in the brief duet in the
finale to Act I, when she realizes the complications that may arise
and seeks to escape from Don Giovanni, fearful and yet fascinated.
To her, more than to Donna Anna and Donna Elvira, is suitable
the sweetness of the delicate legato of the aria "Batti, batti, o bel
Masetto" and the child-like archness of "Vedrai, carino."

Masetto is in the opera as the necessary complement to Zerlina
and as the victim of her deceptions and of Don Giovanni's bullying; but in his aria "Ho capito, signor sì" (probably the last aria
that Mozart composed in Prague before the premiere) also vibrates
a shudder of repressed anger, almost a spirit of rebellion that may
have been more readily received in Prague than in the imperial
capital of Vienna, so closely tied to the life and interests of the
court. Clever comic figures animate his duettino with Zerlina at
the beginning of the finale to Act I, "Presto, presto," newer and
more varied than many of the comic passages in Leporello's more
extensive role.

After the protagonist, Leporello's role is without doubt the most
important in the opera, with regard to the number of scenes and
musical pieces in which he takes part; but despite its breadth and
importance this character is nevertheless most closely modeled in
the mold imposed by tradition. From a certain point of view,
Goldoni had good reasons for depriving his Don Giovanni albeit
in a forced manner) of the inevitable servant; he realized how difficult it would be to abandon the model of Arlecchino or
Scaramuccia or any of the many *zanni* of the commedia dell'arte,
different in name and appearance, but all made from the same

157

substance of greed, gluttony, impudence, and cowardice. Da Ponte could not have had the same scruples; on the contrary, Goldoni's tragicomedy must have shown him that it was impossible to create a comic opera about Don Giovanni (and the opera had to be comic)[39] without the traditional figure of the servant with the characteristics imposed by tradition. With his name, he underlines Leporello's cowardice;[40] neither did he forget to attribute to him venality and gluttony, even though they remain in the background; and impudent is the familiarity with which Leporello does not reprove, but rather reproaches his master's many misdeeds and defines them in more crudely explicit terms. Far from being Don Giovanni's moral conscience, or pseudo-conscience,[41] Leporello is an accomplice, induced to complicity not really out of fear (the innocence "he was robbed of" by his master's bullying is only a convenient alibi), but by his admiration for his adventures, which inspire his fantasy and encourage in him the impulse toward imitation.

If all this regards above all Da Ponte's libretto, even Mozart accepted Leporello as a given, dictated by convention and tradition, indispensable to the opera. Most of Da Ponte's attempts to characterize him, most effectively in his use of words, were destined to be treated in recitative. Aside from recitative, the comedy at the heart of this character often manifests itself in the typical musical style of a comic bass, a puppet-like mechanical style that often approaches that of an instrument placed onstage rather than in the orchestra pit, but used in a way that conforms to characteristic sonorities and traditional conventions (neither more nor less than the basses and bassoons with which his voice is often associated). Fast tempos, easy rhythms, flighty recitatives (often with the rapid repeated notes typical of comic style) suit him, as do the angular melodies that usually embody the harmonic function of the bass line and rarely assume distinctly tuneful characteristics (his tunes are usually imitations of themes already sung by Don Giovanni). Even though this was enough to stimulate Mozart's instrumental and rhythmic invention, there is much more. Leporello begins well with the soliloquy of the poor man who pursues the dream of becoming a great lord, and continues better in the trio that accompanies the Commendatore's death (even though at this point Mozart expresses his own feelings in the presence of the pathos of death more than those of the three characters onstage). Leporello comes out from behind the generic nature of the catalogue aria, in which Mozart succeeds in a miracle of balance and proportion in expressing the satisfying and self-satisfied, exhilarated and exhilarating, complicity of the servant with his master's adventures without indulging in any of the temptations to slip into a roguishly foul-mouthed tone (the same temptation is avoided in a different way in Act II, almost completely passing over his nocturnal ramblings with Donna Elvira). Other brilliant ideas of Mozart's add color to the character in Act II with the sanctimoniousness of his asking pardon in the sextet and the aria "Ah, pietà, signori miei" (in which the dialectic of his self-defense finally entraps him in a series of delightful exchanges between voice and orchestra), and with the abject fear of the graveyard scene (the falling sevenths are a recurrent characteristic of his part) and the finale. But even this attention to the fine points of his psychology, marked by wit and skillfully exploited for effects of contrast, does not suffice to give a human consistency to a character whose traits were fixed so conventionally by tradition.

In the final scene, the two main characters from the preceding scene—the Commendatore and Don Giovanni—are absent. In the opera as a whole, the former occupies a position diametrically opposed to that of Leporello, in view of the part's extreme brevity and the fact that the only two scenes in which he appears are the most intensely dramatic of the entire opera. We vividly recall the effectiveness with which Mozart portrays the violence of the first of these scenes and the way in which Mozart's pity for his death created one of the most moving moments in the opera. But his and our siding with the victim does not suffice to give the character a face; the option of the rapid beginning *in mediis rebus* precludes us from coming to know anything about him other than that he is Donna Anna's father; neither is anything mentioned in what follows about his past as a faithful and honored servant of the crown, which was made clear in Tirso and amplified by Goldoni. When he later returns in the scene before the epilogue, he is a supernatural, dehumanized apparition (we have seen how Mozart's genius conveys his icy inflexibility and the horror that emanates from him) made a passionless instrument of a superior will, not *deus ex machina* but rather *ex coelo machina*.

Don Giovanni is also absent, but even though three characters onstage frankly state they wish to leave him "with Proserpina and Pluto," his memory is still too recent and therefore remains vividly present to all. Donna Elvira's intention to retire to a convent clearly shows the devastation he has wrought in her life. He deprived Donna Anna of an adored father (leaving aside the more subtle and problematic psychological dimensions of this character). He has thrown Don Ottavio's ordered life into confusion and spoiled his rosy prospects of marriage. Zerlina cannot easily forget either the persuasive sweetness of his voice, or the insidious violence that it masked; and Masetto sighs a momentary sigh of relief, but must remain more suspicious than ever of his little wife, as astute as she is fair and given to risky flirtations. Finally, for Leporello it will be easy to find another master at the inn, but not one with whom he can establish the same relationship of admiring and perverse collusion. Don Giovanni, who is responsible for bringing together and intertwining such disparate lives over the course of at least two nights of insanity, is, as the libretto describes him, a "young, extremely licentious cavalier"; but we deceive ourselves if we are satisfied with this preliminary definition, which was intended to be integrated into the action for which it provides a preface. Mozart and Da Ponte certainly inherited a long tradition in which the licentious adventures of the seducer had gradually become the character's most obvious trait; but although they conformed to the tradition, accepting and even exaggerating certain elements ("In Spain, it's already a thousand three"), it was not in the spirit of the time, neither was it in the disposition of the two authors (least of all Da Ponte), to think that his licentiousness justified the terrible exemplary punishment that was also an integral part of the tradition. Also characteristic of their time is the absence of any allusion to atheism, which was underscored in all seventeenth-century interpretations (including Melani's and Acciaiuoli's *Empio punito*); even in the graveyard scene Don Giovanni's impiety consists in his lack of respect for the place and his derision of his victim, which reveals his complete lack of remorse. With Don Giovanni's eroticism therefore are associated more execrable traits, such as arrogance, violence, disdain for the feelings and even the lives of others; it is unnecessary to recount all the episodes in which these traits are shown, except perhaps for the most extreme instance (which also serves as proof of Da Ponte's remarkable dramatic instinct) in which Don Giovanni amuses himself in reasserting his power over Donna Elvira and then throws her into Leporello's arms with sadistic disdain.[42]

Therefore I cannot accept the vitalistic interpretation of Don Giovanni as sinner without having sinned, an insatiably erotic creature whose self-renewing desire necessarily and almost unconsciously leads to violence and cruelty.[43] His refined, perversely intentional cruelty, revives the spirit of Tirso's *Burlador*, shorn of its theological dimensions: the unbridled taste for asserting his power over everyone, every man or woman who has the misfortune to meet him, inflicting suffering and mortification in every way possible. Don Giovanni's greatest sin is his pride, which recognizes no limits to his own pleasure and cruelty, and he cannot repent without denying the very reason for his existence. Don Giovanni coherently unites force, beauty, and insinuating and dangerous sweetness with the inexhaustibly rich resources for transformation of a Lucifer in the heroic grandeur of his fall. Mozart may at first have been attracted to the theme of his adventures (we have seen his comments on this during the preparation of the opera), by the stirring rhythm of his fortunes and his protean transformations, which seem to lend themselves to comic opera. But later, as he identified himself with the happenings in the libretto created by Da Ponte in order to actualize each moment in the music with the vividness and apparent immediacy of his musical ideas, and with the miraculous adaptability of their forms, which he modified according to the dictates of a deep psychological and dramatic intuition, he must have penetrated this fatal difficulty and transcended the limits of their original intention. The grandeur of Mozart's *Don Giovanni*, as in general of all of this composer's work, consists, as Massimo Mila has noted, "in the fact of leading with the greatest skill, effortlessly and without emphasis and grand words, to the threshold of eternal values." But precisely for this reason it is necessary to avoid the term "demonic," so often applied to *Don Giovanni*, which has become so laden with Romantic and post-Romantic significance, emphatic and vaguely allusive. Mozart's *daimon* is what dictates the secure touch and correct intonation to express effortlessly the most disturbing elements in the human spirit.

*　　*　　*

We have left the characters on the point of articulating the conclusion they reach at the end of the epilogue:

E noi tutti, o buona gente,	And let us all, good people,
ripetiam allegramente	Joyfully repeat
l'antichissima canzon.	The age-old song:
Questo è il fin di chi fa mal;	This is the end of him who does evil,
e dei perfidi la morte	And the death of those given to perfidy
alla vita è sempre ugual!	Is always like unto their life!

The first three lines are sung in a jaunty style (ornamented by violins and flutes, while the basses insist on a dominant pedal) by Zerlina, Masetto, and Leporello, the specifically comic characters. Or rather they are sung by singers who have sustained their roles up to this point and who now suddenly divest themselves to address the audience directly, actors to public, as was often the custom in the commedia dell'arte. The idea for this gesture must stem from Da Ponte, to whom it may have been suggested by Gozzi's staged fables; but Mozart must have consented, since he contributed to it with the jesting musical tone of the last three lines, which disperse any trace of the shadow that may remain in the wake of the supernatural catastrophe. The moral of the opera assumes a solemn frown (in the style of "Doctor Gradus ad Parnassum," Debussy's Monsieur Croche would have said) attacking the first line of the "age-old song" like the beginning of a strict fugue; but the theme in D major is agile and brisk, even though notated in long rhythmic values, because of the Presto tempo designation. Under the soft and rapid passage work of the violins, the theme is stated sotto voce by Donna Anna and Donna Elvira; Zerlina answers a fourth lower; and the third statement entrusted to the basses Leporello and Masetto weaves it into a sparkling choral texture that permits the rapid scansion of the last two lines. The voices separate momentarily for a brief dialogue between two groups; then, repeating themselves in a version incorporating a chromatic descent, they cadence sonorously in D major. The last word—or rather gesture, or smile, or nod—is from the violins, which once more softly take up the light figures of the countersubjects that accompanied the fugato subject. It is reassuring to know—or to pretend to know—that the story on which the curtain falls, even with its moments of disturbing brilliance, has not been a fable, and that the ogre's defeat can lead to a moral. We will never know if this is an attempt to reconcile the improbability of the supernatural intervention with the prevailing rationalism of the time, or rather, once more, an oracular pronouncement of Mozart's *daimon*.

NOTES

Chapter One: The Seventeenth Century

1. The passage is reprinted, in the original Latin and in Italian translation, in Macchia, *Vita avventure e morte di Don Giovanni* (Turin: Einaudi, 1978), pp. 109-117.

2. B. Croce, *I teatri di Napoli,* 3rd ed. (Bari: Laterza, 1926), p. 75.

3. Ulisse Prota Giurleo, "Napoli: Stanza di S. Bartolomeo," *Enciclopedia dello spettacolo* (Rome, 1960).

4. It is cited with 1652 as the date of publication in the theatrical bibliography of Leone Allacci (1755 edition), and mentioned by Goldoni in the same context as that by Cicognini; but no exemplars are known today. Croce, *I teatri di Napoli,* p. 78, points to an allusion to *Il convitato di pietra,* evidently already known in some form or other, in *Le pazzie di savi ovvero Il Lambertaccio* (Venice, 1641) by Bartolomeo Bocchini: "Qui tacque il veglio e col suo cor mutato / Rimase senza moto e senza lena, / Che pareva di Pietra il Convitato, / Ma non vi fu chi l'invitasse a cena" ["Here the old man stopped speaking and with a changed heart / Remained motionless, without any will to carry on, / So that he looked like the Stone Guest, / But there was no one to invite him to dinner"].

5. The text is reprinted in Macchia, *Vita avventure,* pp. 167-206. The term "opera" in the subtitle still has the generic meaning of a stage work, without reference to music. The opera libretti by Cicognini are: *Celio* (Florence, music by B. Baglioni and N. Sapiti), *Giasone* (Venice, 1649, music by F. Cavalli), and *Orontea* (Venice, 1649, music by F. Lucio).

6. The most famous is that of *Stellidaura vendicata* (Naples, 1674, music by Francesco Provenzale).

7. Macchia, *Vita avventure*, pp. 119-150.

8. Ibid., pp. 119-135.

9. Notes that survive in a French translation transcribed by Thomas-Simon Gueullette under the title *Le Festin de pierre* and *Suitte du festin de pierre* along with many other texts by this famous Arlecchino; reprinted in Macchia, *Vita avventure,* pp. 161-165.

10. Cf. note 16 below.

11. Cf. the chapter "Lo scenario del Biancolelli" in E. Balmas, *Il mito del Don Giovanni nel Seicento francese* (Rome: Lucarini, 1986), pp. 21-39 (pp. 22-23 quote Boileau's comment on the event). In 1657, the performances were given at the Théâtre du Petit Bourbon, which later formed the first venue of Molière's activity in Paris. Giuseppe Domenico Biancolelli was not yet part of the company; he joined in 1661 and substituted for the leading actor Locatelli upon the latter's death in 1662.

12. See note 11. The text attributed to Biancolelli is a series of notes (rather than a scenario) with details on what the actor should introduce into the part of Don Giovanni's servant, Arlecchino (who is listed first in the cast list).

13. The three comedies along with Molière's are examined in Balmas, *Il mito del Don Giovanni.*

14. Balmas, pp. 96-106, describes the vicissitudes of the two texts and of the Amsterdam edition of 1683 mentioned below.

15. Macchia, *Vita avventure*, pp. 12-14, points out the Italian precedents of this episode; pp. 32-33, note 4, also indicates how this scene was not censored in the Italian translation of the comedy (1697).

16. Sganarelle's witticism has precise precedents that did not provoke the same reactions as those Molière encountered, in the *Convitato* attributed to Cicognini (Passarino: "Oh, my poor master and my wages have gone to the devil!") and in the so-called scenario of Biancolelli (Arlequin: "My wages! I will have to send a bailiff to the devil to get my wages!"); Macchia, *Vita avventure,* pp. 205 and 160, respectively.

17. Macchia, *Vita avventure,* p. 77, note 4, cites the passage in question from A. de Rinaldis, *Lettere inedite di Salvator Rosa a G. B. Ricciardi* (Roma, 1939). In the same note is also cited a later letter dated 2 March 1669 in which Rosa reports of the performance in an unfavorable light: "Last Friday I went to hear the most castrated *Convitato di pietra* [here Rosa may allude to the fact that the part of the protagonist was sung by a soprano castrato], which because of both the heat in the hall and the tediousness of this most solemn nonsense changed my state of mind and increased my bile so strongly that I was forced to stay at home for two days to purge myself. . . . I swear to you that I have never seen such absurdities before, and yet it is entirely the work of our beloved, most excellent Signor Apollonio (but not of Tiana)." From this stems the supposition that Apolloni helped in versifying Acciaiuoli's plot (Apolloni, an old friend of both Rosa's and Ricciardi's, had earlier been Cesti's librettist). Rosa also enjoyed the practice of improvised drama; his letter also confirms the semiprivate nature of the spectacle.

18. The tacit encouragement of the main librettist, Giulio Rospigliosi, whose brief pontificate lasted from June 1666 to December 1669, did not suffice to bring about a revival; it should be noted that the Melani brothers who set Acciaiuoli's libretto to music were, like Rospigliosi, from Pistoia. On theatrical activity in this period see M. Murata, "Il carnevale a Roma sotto Clemente IX," *Rivista italiana di musicologia* 12 (1977): 83-99.

19. A. Ademollo, *I teatri di Roma nel secolo diciassettesimo* (Rome, 1888), pp. 111-12 relates other information about the performance (including the ladies' retaliation) from the manuscript newsletters of the Genoese agent Ferdinando Raggi: 17 February, "This evening they are performing Filippo Acciaiuoli's comedy at the behest of the Queen . . ."; 20 February, "Filippo Acciaiuoli's new comedy has been done at the behest of Donna Caterina [?], who did not want to invite the princesses. Only the ladies . . ."; 23 February, "They say that the Queen . . . did not want a single lady at the comedy that was done the first time at her behest. The Conestabilessa [Maria Mancini Colonna] was there incognito in a box with a little candle in her hand reading the comedy. . . ." (This documents that Teatro Colonna had boxes.) Other theatrical activities are described here, pp. 94-97, but the Teatro Tordinona, which was opened in 1671, is mistakenly mentioned.

20. Ibid., p. 113; the quotation stems from a manuscript newsletter from Rome.

21. Macchia, *Vita avventure*, p. 207.

22. On Acciaiuoli, see F. Fuà, *L'opera di Filippo Acciajuoli* (Fossombrone, 1921) and the entry in the *Dizionario degli italiani*. Robert L. Weaver, "*Il Girello:* A Seventeenth-Century Burlesque Opera," *Quadrivium* 12 (1971): 141-64, which, besides discussing Acciaiuoli, contains source material on various members of the Melani family, all musicians. This material that was later integrated into the same author's "Materiali per le biografie dei fratelli Melani," *Rivista italiana di musicologia* 12 (1977): 252-95. Weaver, "*Il Girello,*" p. 146, speculates that Jacopo Melani (who before settling in Rome had written several Florentine operas) led a company of singers called the "Compagnia del Girello," who were responsible for performances of the opera in various cities from 1668 (after the Roman production) through 1676. Four scores survive for *Girello.* Only one score of *L'empio punito* survives; this work would have been more difficult to export than *Girello* because of the elaborate stage apparatus it required and was never restaged after its Roman production.

23. The two different tendencies are found in the operas based on libretti by Moniglia (in some instances with music by Jacopo Melani) that Acciaiuoli may have come to know during his years in Florence. Among the most famous scenic inventions, Ademollo, *I teatri di Roma,* p. 124, refers to "*La noce di Benevento,* or Witches' Counsel [. . .]. The Elysian Fields in the Teatro Tordinona, and Hell in the Teatro Capranica." Acciaiuoli certainly took part in the management of both theaters. Later he also took his marionette theater to Florence, Turin, and Venice.

24. The interpreter of the role of Bibi must have been the dwarf mentioned in the account of the premiere, related in Ademollo, *I teatri di Roma,* p. 122: "As usual, the dwarf has a good part, a little long, with a touch of melancholy." But where is the melancholy?

25. The complete text of *L'empio punito* is reprinted in Macchia, *Vita avventure,* pp. 207-299.

26. Ibid., p. 209.

27. Weaver, "*Il Girello,*" p. 145. [Translator's note: for the evidence of Alessandro Melani's *Ergenia* (Rome, carnival 1668), see Robert L. Weaver, "Alessandro Melani," *New Grove Dictionary of Opera* (London: Macmillan, 1992).]

28. Murata, "Il carnevale," p. 95, note 31, relates from the Sistine diaries (6 January 1669): "During carnival, Signori Giuseppe Fede and Francesco Verdoni also have permission from his Eminence Rospigliosi to be involved in the opera on days other than feast days."

29. See note 24.

Chapter Two: The Eighteenth Century

1. L. A. Muratori, *Della perfetta poesia italiana,* ed. A. Rusconi (Milan: Marzorati, 1971), vol. 2, pp. 571-572. The original edition of the treatise was published in Modena in 1706.

2. Ibid., p. 272.

3. On Zeno's activity as a librettist, see E. Sala di Felice, "Zeno: da Venezia a Vienna," *L'opera italiana a Vienna prima di Metastasio,* ed. M. T. Muraro (Florence: Olschki, 1990), pp. 65-114.

4. In *Lettere di Apostolo Zeno cittadino veneziano istorico e poeta cesareo* (Venice, 1785), vol. 1, p. 56. The letter dated 6 August 1701 and addressed to Muratori was cited by the latter to support his theses. Later Zeno (in a letter from Vienna dated 3 November 1730, vol. 4, pp. 277-279), while still *poeta cesareo* (though but for a little while longer), argued that Muratori's judgement, which he had earlier approved of, was too severe; but another letter (dated 27 December 1735, vol. 5, pp. 152-153) again condemns the genre and his own "abortions and deformities."

5. There are various modern editions of *Il teatro alla moda* (the title's reference to "fashionable theater" is meant ironically).

6. Sala di Felice provides examples, including at the end, p. 114, a list of the operas indicating the virtue that each one emphasizes. See also G. Gronda, *La carriera di un librettista: Pietro Pariati* (Reggio Emilia, 1990), and K. Leich, *Girolamo Frigimelica Roberti* (Munich, 1972).

7. It should be recalled that throughout the seventeenth century, as in earlier centuries, stage performances took place without interruption from beginning to end with the passage from one act to another indicated in seventeenth-century operas for the most part through danced intermezzi (as seen in *L'empio punito*). As a consequence, all changes of scene,

including those from one act to the next, were marvels of stage technique that took place before the spectators' eyes, since the curtain remained open from the beginning to the end of the spectacle. The increase in the number of acts doubled the number of intermezzi from two to four increasing the length and cost of the spectacle.

8. Aside from W. Binni, *L'arcadia e il Metastasio* (Florence: La Nuova Italia, 1963), I would draw particular attention to the following contributions to the literature on Metastasio: L. Ronga, "L'opera metastasiana," in P. Metastasio, *Opere* (Milan-Naples, 1968), and the more recent volumes of E. Sala di Felice, *Metastasio: ideologia, drammaturgia, spettacolo* (Milan: Angeli, 1983) and J. Joly, *Dagli Elisi all'inferno* (Florence: La Nuova Italia, 1990).

9. Metastasio was largely unhappy with the Viennese settings of his libretti, particularly those by Caldara, who belonged to the older generation. Metastasio's tastes were formed by the works of younger composers belonging to the Neapolitan school whom he had met during his Italian period, mainly Sarro, Porpora, and Vinci. Later he also came to appreciate Jommelli and Hasse. See my article, "I musicisti nell'epistolario di Metastasio," in *Scelte poetiche di musicisti* (Venice: Marsilio, 1987), pp. 277-289.

10. Contributing to this is the increased disparity between the recitative dialogue and the arias, which is usually attributed to the growing influence of bel canto and virtuoso singers. But I attribute it also to the tendency among composers toward broader musical forms, parallel to developments in the field of instrumental music; see N. Pirrotta, "Metastasio e il terminare le scene con spirito e vivezza," in the course of publication in a collection of studies in honor of Gianfranco Folena.

11. In this regard, Goldoni's account of his first attempt at libretto writing (in the preface to vol. 11 of the Pasquali edition of his works) is of interest. A patient listener counseled him to follow the example of the "profound Zeno" and the "mellifluous Metastasio" to learn "the rules, which, to be sure, were contrary to those of Aristotle and Horace and all those who had written about the art of poetry, but necessary to serve the music,

the actors and the composers. . . . The first soprano [a male], the prima donna, and the tenor, who are the principal actors in the drama, must sing five arias each, one pathetic, the other bravura, one parlante, one di *mezzo carattere* and one brilliant. The *secondo uomo* and *seconda donna* must have four each, and the last singer three, and the same for the seventh singer, if the opera requires one. . . . The fifteen arias of the first singers must be distributed in such a way that two of the same type do not follow one another; the arias of the other singers serve to provide chiaroscuro." It was against the rules "to make a character who remains on stage sing"; instead arias were usually sung by characters who were taking leave of the others to exit the stage.

12. It is well known that the development of bel canto and the idolizing of great virtuosos degenerated into the bad habit of the Italian opera-going public, disenchanted with regard to novelty in libretti (often already heard in different musical settings), of conversing and playing games in their boxes during recitatives (another attraction of opera was that of being a social event). The arias of the minor characters were also often ignored, from which derives the habit of referring to such arias as "arie del sorbetto" ["sorbet arias"].

13. C. E. Troy, *The Comic Intermezzo* (Ann Arbor: UMI Research Press, 1979), pp. 36-37, lists the earliest documented "Independent Venetian Intermezzi (1706–1709)." This book, which is the work of a late lamented student of mine, admirably brings together information on both well known and obscure intermezzi.

14. The proximity of the production of this opera and the year of publication of Benedetto Marcello's *Il teatro all moda* should be noted. The following also satirize the world of the theater: *Chi non fa non falla* by Buini (1732) and *Le metamorfosi odiamorose in birba trionfante nelle gare delle terre amanti,* Antonio Rigo's caricature of a *dramma per musica,* produced in 1732 in Venice and Padua with the music of Salvatore Apolloni. But it is inaccurate to maintain, as some have, that this is a theme characteristic of Venetian or North Italian comic opera; it suffices to recall the Roman and Neapolitan intermezzi *La Dirindina* by Domenico Scarlatti and Metastasio's *La cantatrice e l'impresario* (for *Didone abbandonata* of 1724),

or *La cantarina, commedia pe' mmuseca* (librettist and composer unknown), produced at the Neapolitan Teatro dei Fiorentini in 1728.

15. The Teatro San Fantin, in which various comic operas appeared in the three years from 1717 through 1719 (after which it was closed), was the smallest theater in Venice. The theaters that produced comic operas in the years that followed often did so during the Ascension Day Fair, which attracted many foreigners to Venice. Later on, as the frequency of comic operas came close to equaling that of serious operas, the choice of operas for Ascensiontide would fall on serious operas as often as comic.

16. The Teatro San Giovanni Grisostomo ceased to present operas almost completely after 1751, for reasons that will be discussed below in connection with Goldoni's *Don Giovanni Tenorio.*

17. Mozart does this in the thematic catalogue he compiled of his own works, which he began in February 1784 and continued through 15 November 1791 (three weeks before his death), recently republished as W.A. Mozart, *Verzeichnis aller meiner Werke,* ed. E. H. Müller von Asow (Wien-Wiesbaden, 1956).

18. Taddeo Wiel, *I teatri veneziani nel Settecento* (Venice, 1897), nos. 895 and 896 (1779), 920 (1781), 932 (1782), and 1026 (1788).

19. Produced at the Teatro San Moisè in Venice in 1751, it also bears the subtitle *tragedia tragichissima ma di lieto fine* (text by Giovanni Fiorini, music by Gaetano Latilla); it was restaged in Amsterdam in 1753 with the title *L'opera in prova alla moda, dramma giocoso.* The 1753 edition has a preface indicating that the so-called tragedy was presented as a play within a play; in fact, the work consists of a rehearsal followed by a performance.

20. Cerlone's *Il nuovo convitato di pietra* cannot be considered a work with literary intent. S. Kunze, *Don Giovanni vor Mozart* (Munich: Fink, 1972), pp. 29 ff., has drawn attention to the work. The lack of literary intent is clear from the buffo style, the use of Neapolitan dialect, and the fact that one scene is even left to improvisation ("Dottore and Trappola perform a comic scene").

21. Critics have associated this group of early works, under the label "tragi-comedy," with another series of works (most of them with exotic subject matter) that Goldoni began in 1753 with *La sposa persiana.* Actually, Goldoni only labelled the later series "tragicomedies"; of the earlier ones he labelled "tragedies" those with historical subject matter, and "comedies" those, like *Don Giovanni Tenorio,* with romance-genre plots at times pointing out, however, the possibility of considering them tragicomedies.

22. Cf. Goldoni's statements in the preface to vol. 1 of the Bettinelli edition (Venice, 1750): "Tragedies and *drammi per musica* presented by commedia dell'arte performers have sustained the theater. In fact, our worthy actors have performed excellent tragedies and beautiful *drammi* with praiseworthy form and have succeeded admirably. What success have the *drammi* of the celebrated *abate* Metastasio and those of the illustrious Zeno not enjoyed . . . , and have not some of my own productions enjoyed some approval? that is, *Belisario, Rosmonda, Don Giovanni Tenorio,* . . . although I do not dare call them tragedies, since I know them to be defective in many parts."

23. Here the Italian text uses the word "opera" to refer to any theatrical work, which was the most generic sense it bore in the theatrical jargon of the day.

24. Carlo Goldoni, *Tutte le opere,* ed. G. Ortolani (Milan, 1950), vol. 9, pp. 214-215.

25. The names "Carino," "Montano," and "Silvio" were probably suggested by Guarini's *Il pastor fido;* the name "Megacle," which is not actually pastoral, is taken from Metastasio's *Olimpiade,* where Megacle is the alter ego of Licida. "Licisca" may be a mistaken form of "Licida," or more likely a conflation of "Licida" and "Corisca" (the meddling nymph whose conduct is far from impeccable in *Il pastor fido,* and who resembles Goldoni's Elisa).

26. Evidently Goldoni was unable to avoid the incongruity of the "marble statue erected in a few moments," even though it neither speaks, nor walks, nor exchanges invitations to dinner, nor serves as the instrument of divine vengeance.

27. Goldoni's afore-mentioned dedication contains interesting points of consideration with regard to theatrical conditions: "Today the condition of musical theater throughout Italy is terminal. . . . . Foreign courts hire the best subjects of our country . . . and those who remain take advantage of the favorable opportunity to demand a great deal. At present, comedies enjoy the largest audiences; and comic operas give delight at little expense." The greater cost of *opera seria* therefore contributed to the flourishing of comic opera, a situation that forced Grimani to suspend opera at the Teatro San Giovanni Grisostomo.

28. The question of precedence contested by Angiolini and Noverre remains unresolved: *Le Festin de pierre* was the first dramatization of dance, but Noverre had already treated the dramatization of dance theoretically a year earlier in his *Lettres sur la danse*. Angiolini also criticized Noverre's plot descriptions as too minutely detailed, maintaining that music and dance should suffice to transmit to spectators the meaning of the ballet's action.

29. This passage and the quotations that follow are originally in French, the language the program was written in, as well as an indication of the orientation toward French culture which characterized the phase of Viennese theatrical activity that unfolded under the auspices of Count Durazzo.

30. With this phrase, Angiolini attempts to counter the accusations of lack of verisimilitude directed toward the actions of the statue, an example of which we have seen in Goldoni's criticisms.

31. Related by R. Haas, *Gluck und Durazzo im Burgtheater* (Zürich, 1925), p. 67; Zinzendorf's diary also is in French.

32. It is often claimed that the plot of *Le Festin* derives from the plot of Molière's comedy; actually the only notable point of contact is the name "Donna Elvira," who, however, in *Le Festin* is the daughter of the Commendatore, and Don Giovanni's lover, and therefore the equivalent of Donna Anna.

33. For the sources of the two versions and an examination of their contents, see R. Engländer's introduction to his edition of the ballet in C. W. Gluck, *Sämtliche Werke* (Kassel, 1966), vol. 2, p. 1.

34. No. 13 can be related to nos. 1 and 18, as a characterization of the protagonist. No. 7 is entitled "Gavotte." In others one can glimpse dances, flights, tempests, and declarations of love. The numbers added to the end of Act II may correspond to comic actions on the part of Don Giovanni's servant.

35. The same concepts are repeated in the program of *Semiramis,* "tragédie en ballet pantomime" (1765), also to Gluck's music; here Angiolini writes about this work: "If I succeed I must share the honor of success with him." The score of *Semiramis* also contains an overture and fifteen pieces.

36. He was not among the musicians who met with the poet's favor. In response to the Viennese performances of *Semiramide riconosciuta* (1748), Metastasio wrote: " . . . it reaches the stars thanks to the excellence of the company and the magnificence of the stage sets, in spite of the music of that arch-Vandal"; see Pirrotta, *Scelte poetiche di musicisti,* p. 284.

37. The literature on Gluck and his reform of opera is vast. For my present purposes, I will point to P. Gallarati, *Gluck e Mozart* (Turin: Einaudi, 1973).

38. Macchia, *Vita avventure,* pp. 39-40.

39. Here I adopt the title of Kunze's book, cited above.

40. Le Tellier's *Festin de pierre,* produced in 1713 at the Saint Germain Fair in Paris, is sometimes mentioned in this context. This could not have been a true *opéra comique* but rather, as usual in the stage works at the Paris fairs, a spoken comedy with intermezzi of vaudeville songs, that is songs on popular topics. More noble was certainly, at the end of the seventeenth century (1692), Purcell's incidental music for *The Libertine* by Thomas Shadwell. To return to *La pravità castigata,* only one copy of the

libretto survives, which is in Italian with the German translation on facing pages; Kunze, *Don Giovanni vor Mozart*, tables 1 and 2, reproduces the frontispiece, the list of characters and singers, and the letter to the reader.

41. Their career as impresarios, which began precisely here in Brünn (1732–1736) continued over the course of twenty years in Graz, Hamburg, Prague, Linz, Frankfurt, Leipzig, Dresden, Copenhagen, Lübeck; see E. H. Müller, *Angelo e Pietro Mingotti* (Dresden, 1917), and P. Nettl, "Pietro e Angelo Mingotti," *Enciclopedia dello spettacolo*.

42. She had performed secondary roles in *opere serie;* that she assumed the protagonist's role in *La pravità castigata* indicates that she was a better actress than she was a singer and therefore adapted to the comic repertoire; the same can be said of Laura Bambini, who may have been the composer's sister (who performed the dual role of Don Garzia and Donna Beatrice). Chiara Orlandi (King Manfredi) may have been a better singer; she appeared in Venice in 1717 and beginning in 1720 styled herself "virtuosa di S. A. Ser. il Duca di Massa e Carrara" (but she is no longer labeled as such in the libretto of *La pravità*). See Wiel, *I teatri musicali veneziani*, passim.

43. Peruzzi had sung in Venice from 1724 through 1733, at times in roles of some importance; see Wiel, *I teatri*. She must have been related to Pietro Denzio, an impresario in Venice in 1715-1716, and Antonio Denzio, a singer in Venice from 1715 through 1720 and impresario in Prague from 1723 through 1734, and later sporadically elsewhere. Cecilia Monti and Bartolomeo Cajo are not mentioned in Wiel's indices, perhaps because libretti rarely indicate the performers of the comic intermezzi; but Monti is often listed as a singer in intermezzi in the various cities in which companies directed by the Mingotti brothers performed.

44. See R. Meloncelli, "Eustachio Bambini," *Dizionario biografico degli italiani*. He was *maestro di cappella* in Cortona and later in Pesaro through 1734. There is no evidence that he was ever connected with the Viennese court.

45. This is the label for operas with music by various composers, particularly frequent in the eighteenth century as the result either of an initial distribution of the task of composition among various composers, or modifications, interpolations, and substitutions introduced in the course of new productions in various theaters. In this instance, it seems that Bambini incorporated the music of others as he wrote his score.

46. Kunze, *Don Giovanni vor Mozart,* p. 28.

47. Libretti pointed out by Kunze, *Don Giovanni vor Mozart,* p. 74, together with indications of other performances in Brunswick in 1782-1783.

48. Kunze, *Don Giovanni vor Mozart,* pp. 74-77.

49. In Vienna, a manuscript copy of the score stemming from Eszterháza and therefore with revisions that may derive from Haydn survives along with scores of the Act II and Act III finales.

50. The finale to Act I seems to include the murder of the Commendatore and a final aria for Donna Anna; the finale to Act II is Don Giovanni's dinner; the finale to Act III consists of the chorus of the Furies, to which, however, was added in Vienna a comic scene between Arlecchino and Corallina.

51. Albertini had an intermezzo of his performed in Rome in 1772. After moving to Poland in the service of Prince Radziwill and later at the court in Warsaw, he composed *opere serie* almost exclusively. His *Don Giovanni* was labelled *opera semiseria.*

52. Kunze, *Don Giovanni vor Mozart,* underlines the unusual orchestration in the context of a comic opera (but this was also a court performance) as well as the pathos of several scenes, and transcribes the music for the death of the Commendatore in an appendix, pp. 207-210.

53. He produced an opera there in 1770 and after *Il convitato* produced two other operas in Modena and Venice in 1779 and 1782. His brother Antonio (1757-1828) began his career as an opera composer in Venice in

1782. For their activity as impresarios, see B. Brunelli, *I teatri di Padova* (Padua, 1921).

54. See N. Mangini, *I teatri di Venezia* (Milan: Mursia, 1973), pp. 98-104.

55. Wiel, *I teatri,* p. 331.

56. Nunziato Porta, Righini's librettist, may already have arrived there. In 1778, Porta appeared as the librettist of two comic operas produced at the Teatro San Samuele.

Chapter Three: Mozart's Immediate Antecedents

1. I pointed to this in the preceding chapter. Kunze, *Don Giovanni vor Mozart,* pp. 39-42, relates that this comedy is present only in the Bolognese 1789 edition of the works of Cerlone and is absent from the Neapolitan editions of 1772, 1775, and 1825–1829.

2. *La scuffiara* was set by Paisiello in 1787 under the title of *La modista raggiratrice* [The Swindling Milliner], but had already appeared with Tritto's music in 1784.

3. Lorenzi and his comedies are amply documented in M. Scherillo, *L'opera buffa napoletana durante il Settecento* (Palermo, 1930); see also V. Monaco, *Giambattista Lorenzi e la commedia per musica* (Naples, 1968). Having distinguished himself in his collaborations in theatrical activities in the houses of various nobles, he joined the company of the court theater in 1763 and became its director in 1769. His activity as a prolific and spirited poet contrasts with the severity he later showed others in his exercise of his responsibilities of royal censor of operas. His most successful works have received praise for the at least partial renunciation of dialect, the use of a type of comedy free of excessive vulgarity, and in the last phase of his career the emphasis on sentiment, which derives from

French *comédie larmoyante* (*Nina pazza per amore* is one example of this); but he was also capable of opportunistically deviating from these goals, as *Il convitato* shows, to indulge in effects of immediate popularity.

4. Born in Puglia, Tritto lived in Naples from the time he was a boy, studying music at the Conservatorio della Pietà dei Turchini, to which he remained attached for the rest of his life, advancing slowly from the position of *maestrino* (student teacher), to *secondo maestro straordinario* in 1785, *secondo maestro* in 1793, and finally *primo maestro* in 1799; he continued to teach counterpoint and composition there until his death. Today, he is remembered for numbering among his students composers who would later enjoy a great deal of fame, such as Spontini, Bellini, and Mercadante. At first, he had few opportunities to prove himself as a composer, despite one opera written for the Teatro dei Fiorentini when he was barely twenty-one years old; even the petition he addressed to the king in 1772 to be permitted to write an opera for the Teatro San Carlo was rejected. Therefore the sudden fervor of his operatic activity (for the most part comic and often consisting of works in one act) is surprising; it began in 1780 with a *Principe riconosciuto* and continued with alacrity over the the course of two decades, only slackening off with the beginning of the new century. On Tritto, see G. De Napoli, *La triade melodrammatica altamurana* (Milan, 1931).

5. This passage is cited more fully in Scherillo, *L'opera buffa napoletana*, p. 369, where, however, the same *Infedeltà fedele* is criticized as a *pastorelleria bislacca*, in which "there is even a character who, forgetting that he lives in the times of the goddess Diana, slobbers over a certain Frenchman who affects Neapolitan airs to get him to believe that he is a nobleman."

6. Croce, *I teatri di Napoli*, pp. 241-42, devotes some attention to Coltellini (in the context of a chapter nominally dedicated to Lorenzi) and praises her good manners and conduct, in contrast to the faults of other singers, qualities which will lead after her brief career to a happy marriage with a Swiss banker.

7. In a later version, found in the complete edition of Lorenzi's works published in Naples beginning in 1806 (the version reprinted in

Monaco, *G.B. Lorenzi,* pp. 463-513), the interventions of Isabella and the minister are cut and new dialogues between Lesbina and her father are introduced. (In this later version, the minister is a governor; though mentioned, he never appears.)

8. Although this manuscript is labeled an autograph by both a stamp that appears repeatedly on its pages, and by the stamp of the library of the Conservatorio di musica S. Pietro a Majella, in Naples, which owns the manuscript, it is actually in several hands, only one of which could possibly be Tritto's. The frontispiece refers to the production of 1783, but the manuscript shows signs of reworking connected to other productions: the role of Chiarella, whose text in dialect is augmented by new text in Italian; some passages modified by the censors; and the two versions of the final scene, the first of which eliminates the vision of the "Ghost representing the damned Don Giovanni," which is present in the libretto of 1783.

9. The score also varies with regard to instrumentation. In the introduction, the oboes are doubled by clarinets and in one aria trumpets replace horns. M.F. Robinson, *Naples and Neapolitan Opera* (Oxford, 1972), p. 161, relates that the orchestra at the Teatro dei Fiorentini toward the close of the seventeenth century consisted of twenty-three players.

10. M.F. Robinson, p. 175.

11. A bit of buffoonery already present in Calegari's opera (see above) and certainly deriving from the improvisations of the commedia dell'arte.

12. The sets are, in order: "City with the Commendatore's palace to one side and a practicable balcony," "Countryside with rustic abodes," "Chamber" (in the home of the Marcquis Dorasquez), "City," "Temple with the Commendatore's equestrian statue," "Atrium of the temple," "Chamber in the home of the Marchese," and finally "Temple with table covered in mourning, with black candles and candelabras, and strewn with serpents, frogs, and other poisonous animals" (to which is added a vision of "hell"). Even though it begins by alternating a deep set with a shallow one (made up of a simple backdrop behind which one could prepare the following

deep set), the rapidity of set changes may have required that more than one shallow set be used between the deep ones.

13. The word "clarinets" is added in another hand to the indication of the oboe parts at the beginning of the finale (folio 125 of the score).

14. Among the purely verbal variants are the changes made to the words of the Marquis whenever he mentions a king. These must correspond to the establishment of the Parthenopean Republic at the end of the century. Among those that regard the music is the revision of the finale, whose text beginning with f. 159*v* no longer corresponds to the libretto and eliminates the vision of hell and Don Giovanni's ghost (at various points in this finale the notation consists of the vocal parts alone and the instrumental parts are left blank). The original finale, still lacking several transitional measures, begins again on f. 164.

15. On these productions, see Kunze, *Don Giovanni vor Mozart,* pp. 87-90, which also relates a piece from the translation and reworking used by Fabrizi. He also cites, pp. 113 ff., several productions of Gazzaniga's opera (see below) whose libretti indicate interpolations of Fabrizi's music.

16. Several scholars refer to him as Neapolitan, but the libretto of *I tre gobbi rivali,* published in Naples, refers to him as Roman (see also the note that follows). O. G. T. Sonneck, *Library of Congress Catalogue of Opera Librettos* (Washington, 1914), vol. 1, p. 1091, states that only part of the music turns out to be by Fabrizi, who, however, is the only composer mentioned.

17. There is also some uncertainty as to the date of this production, but Kunze, *Don Giovanni vor Mozart,* p. 87, cites a manuscript libretto at the Nationalbibliothek in Vienna that reads "Musica del Sig. Vincenzo Fabrizj, Mro di Cappella Romano 1787 Roma al Teatro Valle nell'Autunno."

18. The libretto bears no indication of the city of publication, neither is it clear what city the Teatro de' due Muri was located in.

19. Macchia, *Vita avventure,* p. 76, gives the name of Giuseppe Foppa as librettist, but does not indicate whether this is a matter of conjecture or based upon secure documentation. Gardi had begun his career as a librettist in Venice only a year earlier with a *dramma serio;* his later activity, often associated in his comic vein with Foppa, was of almost exclusively local interest. There are succinct narrations of the plot of the two acts in Macchia, pp. 86-87, and Kunze, *Don Giovanni vor Mozart,* pp. 82-87, the first with some references to the score, which survives in a unique copy in the library of the Civico museo bibliografico musicale of Bologna (formerly known as the library of the Liceo musicale).

20. The text of both acts of *Il capriccio drammatico* is reprinted in Kunze, *Don Giovanni vor Mozart,* pp. 140-187; all commentators that have focused on the most direct antecedent to Mozart's opera speak diffusely of the *Don Giovanni* libretto here. See, in particular, the comparisons drawn in Macchia, *Vita avventure,* pp. 88 ff.

21. "Informato mi son, caro Impresario: / che la volete dar per cosa nuova, / ed è vecchia all'opposto / più ancor dell'invenzion del Menarosto. / La fanno i Commedianti / da due secoli in quà con del schiamazzo, / ma solamente per il popolazzo." ["I have become aware, my dear impresario, / That you would like to pass it as something new / Quite to the contrary—it is old, / Even older than the invention of Menarosto. / The commedia dell'arte players have done it / For two centuries now with a great deal of brawling, / Though only for the rabble"].

22. Kunze, *Don Giovanni vor Mozart,* pp. 129 ff., lists all the libretti for the restagings of Gazzaniga's opera. Those for the productions at Milan and Turin of 1789, separated and catalogued individually in several libraries, contributed to the erroneous attribution of a setting of *Don Giovanni* to Cimarosa. In *L'impresario in angustie,* a theatrical troupe also finds itself in difficulties, above all because of the disputes arising from jealousy and professional rivalry among the *prima buffa,* the *prima donna giocosa,* and the *prima donna seria,* disputes that eventually induce the impresario to leave everyone in the lurch. In the original version, everything ends with a loving reconciliation between the *prima buffa* and the poet, with nothing to prepare the performance of a second act; only at La Scala in 1789

is this situation remedied by the substitution of a finale for the love duet, in which everyone accepts the poet's suggestion: "Zitto: facciam così: uniamci tutti, / recitiamo a carato: / facciamo il Convitato: che ne dite?" ["Hush! Let's do this: Let's all unite, / And come together / To put on *The Stone Guest*. What do you say?"]

23. The claim that this work had already been performed in Vienna in 1780 thanks to Salieri's support cannot be accurate: Da Ponte had not yet contemplated writing libretti by this time; neither is it probable that Gazzaniga had any contact with Salieri, nor that Salieri had sufficient authority to recommend him. But in 1774 *La donna soldato* had already been performed in Vienna, *La Contessa di Nuovaluna* (1778) and *La donna capricciosa* (1780) in Dresden, and *La vivandiera* in Berlin (to mention only the works of Gazzaniga that were first performed outside Italy).

24. The libretto of *Il capriccio drammatico* claims that "the music is completely new by several masters," but the music of Act I is probably still, in whole or in part, that of Alessandri.

25. Kunze, *Don Giovanni vor Mozart,* p. 30.

26. In Act I of *Il capriccio drammatico*, the third lady, Elisabetta Marchesini, sang a minor role, that of Calandra, with one aria; in *Don Giovanni,* her part is extremely brief.

27. He enjoyed greater success in serious than in comic roles. In Act I of *Il capriccio drammatico,* he was assigned only one aria; he also has a single aria in the act by Gazzaniga, in scene iv, after which he only has brief passages in a recitative and in the final scene. Mozart made effective use of him in duets, ensembles, and in one lovely aria.

28. It would have to have been addressed to the German city in which the action was taking place (a city that is not precisely indicated).

29. He is a tenor.

30. After Bertati's original text, Kunze, *Don Giovanni vor Mozart,* pp. 188-204, indicates Da Ponte's numerous interventions, which without directly drawing upon his earlier words at times resembles the text he wrote for Mozart.

31. There is a certain discrepancy between the musical form and the distribution of the strophes of the text.

32. One can perhaps recognize a vague resemblance between the second part and the opening passages of the two serenades Mozart assigns to Don Giovanni, the one addressed to Donna Elvira, which also is a dissimulation, and the other addressed to Donna Elvira's chambermaid, who never appears on stage.

33. This is noted in the unpublished piano-vocal score edited by Guido Turchi for a performance by Radiotelevisione Italiana, p. 134.

34. In 1783, he had two operas performed there, one each at the Teatro dei Fiorentini and the Teatro del Fondo.

35. Kunze, *Don Giovanni vor Mozart,* p. 96, compares the two passages. However, he does not take into account that the two composers arrive at the new key from opposite directions, Gazzaniga from the key of E-flat, Mozart from the key of F.

36. In a letter to the *abate* Galiani written from Saint Petersburg in 1781, these are the requests that Paisiello asked be transmitted to the librettist preparing the text of *Il barbiere di Siviglia:* "very little recitative. . . . They want as many musical pieces as possible, arias, cavatinas, duets, trios, and finales that occur in the course of the action in the Neapolitan style." I cite this letter from A. Della Corte, *Paisiello* (Turin, 1922), pp. 70-72.

37. The only difference in this regard between the introductions of Gazzaniga and Mozart is that the former introduces a rhythmic acceleration and maintains it even during the death agonies, while Mozart closes the last episode with an Andante of great expressive intensity.

Chapter Four: Mozart and Da Ponte

1. The bibliography on Mozart is vast. Among the relatively recent and more accessible monographs, I would cite: A. Einstein, *Mozart: His Character, His Work*, trans. Arthur Mendel and Nathan Broder (London: Cassell, 1966); B. Paumgartner, *Mozart*, 6th ed. (Freiburg i. B.: Atlantis, 1967); A. Greither, *Mozart* (Turin: Einaudi, 1968; with a catalogue of Mozart's works); W. Hildesheimer, *Mozart*, trans. Marion Faber (New York: Farrar, Straus, Giroux, 1982); and finally G. Carli Ballola and R. Parenti, *Mozart* (Milan: Rusconi, 1990). With regard to Mozart's operas, I have already cited Kunze, *Mozarts Opern* (Stuttgart: Philipp Reclam, 1984).

2. "Singspiel," literally "sung play," has come to be adopted as the generic label for German stage works, especially from the second half of the eighteenth century, that, like English ballad operas and French *opéras comiques* (upon which they were modeled), alternated sung pieces with spoken dialogue.

3. *Serenata, festa teatrale,* and similar terms designate brief, usually celebratory stage works; e.g., *Ascanio in Alba* was performed to celebrate the wedding of Archduke Ferdinand to Maria Beatrice of Modena.

4. It was later translated into German and performed as a singspiel in various German cities.

5. On Da Ponte, see A. Fitzlyon, *The Libertine Librettist* (London: Calder, 1955); F. D'Amico, "Lorenzo Da Ponte," *Enciclopedia dello spettacolo;* G. Scarabello, "Lorenzo Da Ponte," *Dizionario biografico degli italiani*. P. Lecaldano in L. Da Ponte, *Tre libretti per Mozart* (Milan: Rizzoli, 1956), pp. 5-48, presents information on his life and his collaboration with Mozart.

6. Einstein, *Mozart* (New York: Oxford University Press), pp. 460-61. The protagonist of *Il re Teodoro* (an actual historical personage, who was for a brief time king of Corsica and ended his life in exile) is, with more cordial and generous traits, a precursor of the characters of Mozart's *Don Giovanni. La villanella rapita* anticipates the theme of social criticism in *Le nozze di Figaro.*

7. Beaumarchais's five acts were criticized and censured at length before reaching the stage. At the end of a long preface, the author provides the following summary: "The most playful and ingenuous plot in the world: a great lord in love with a girl and resolved to seduce her, and her efforts, those of her fiancé, and of the wife of the lord to frustrate the designs of an absolute lord, who is omnipotent in his social station, wealth, and prodigality. There you have it all, and nothing more. . . ." The comedy is the second part of a trilogy, the first part of which, *Le Barbier de Seville,* had already been used as an operatic theme in Paisiello's *Il barbiere di Siviglia,* which had already been staged in Vienna in 1783.

8. Da Ponte, *Tre libretti per Mozart,* p. 53.

9. The single reference to Da Ponte is in a letter to his father from Vienna dated 7 May 1783: "Here as poet we have a certain *abate* Da Ponte. At the moment, he is awfully busy. . . . He has promised to write a new piece for me, but who knows if he can and will keep his word." For Mozart's original text see Mozart, *Briefe und Aufzeichnungen: Gesamtausgabe,* eds. Wilhelm A. Bauer and Otto Erich Deutsch, vol. 3 (Kassel: Bärenreiter, 1963), pp. 267-69, letter no. 745. For the standard English translation see Emily Anderson, *The Letters of Mozart and His Family* (New York: W. W. Norton, 1989), pp. 847-48.

10. L. Da Ponte, *Memorie* (Milan: Rizzoli, 1960), pp. 108-109.

11. Da Ponte, *Memorie,* recounts the difficulties he encountered because the emperor had forbidden the German actors from performing Beaumarchais's work, and how he himself persuaded his sovereign to lift the ban for Mozart's opera; among Joseph II's objections was that "Mozart, most excellent as an instrumental composer, has only ever written one

opera, and that one was no big deal!" This lack of confidence may also explain the limited success of *Le nozze di Figaro.*

12. Letter of 15 January 1787 to Gottfried von Jacquin. For Mozart's original see Mozart, *Briefe und Aufzeichnungen,* vol. 3, pp. 9-12, letter no. 1022. For an English translation see Anderson, pp. 902-5.

13. She was the daughter of the librettist Marco Coltellini, who also was well known in Vienna, where he had resided since 1772, and to Mozart, with whom he had collaborated in 1772 and 1774. Emperor Joseph II had heard her sing in Naples in 1783 and had suggested that she be invited to Vienna; he held in high esteem of her musicality, expressivity, and ability as a performer.

14. Da Ponte, *Tre libretti per Mozart,* p. 211.

15. See A. Della Corte, *Paisiello,* pp. 70-72. I have referred to this letter above.

16. See F. Chrysander, "Die Opern *Don Giovanni* von Gazzaniga und von Mozart," *Vierteljahrschrift für Musikwissenschaft* 4 (1888): 381 ff; H. Abert, *W. A. Mozart* (Leipzig, 1919–1921), vol. 2, p. 450; G. de Saint-Foix, *W. A. Mozart* (Paris, 1946), vol. 4, pp. 268-ff.; E. J. Dent, *Mozart's Operas* (London, 1947), pp. 129 ff. Also M. Mila, *Lettura del Don Giovanni di Mozart* (Turin: Einaudi, 1988), adheres to this prejudice. Kunze, *Don Giovanni vor Mozart,* pp. 59-71, also follows these lines in his detailed comparison of the two libretti.

17. Beyond these considerations, no one has ever taken into account the many repercussions of the story of the punished libertine in German theater.

18. *Il finto cieco,* to a libretto by Da Ponte, was performed there in 1786. It should be noted, with regard to *Don Giovanni* by Bertati and Gazzaniga, that the tenor Antonio Baglioni who performed the role of Don Ottavio later created the same role in Mozart's opera.

19. One for Salieri who "had written the music of the opera *Tarar* [sic, recte *Tarare,* to a text by Beaumarchais] in Paris, and wanted to reduce it to the style of Italian music and drama, and therefore asked me for a free translation"; one for Martin y Soler, "adaptable to his sweetest melodies"; and the third for Mozart, for whom Da Ponte says he chose "*Don Giovanni,* a subject that pleases him immeasurably." Thus Da Ponte, *Memorie,* pp. 127-28, refers to these libretti, but in his subsequent discussion, instead of relating the information we would like to have on how his work proceeded with Mozart, he describes at length his relationship with a "lovely young girl" whose face was "always smiling, always gay and created expressly to inspire poetic fancy and witty ideas."

20. Dent, *Mozart's Operas,* pp. 138 ff. According to Dent, Act I would have ended with Donna Anna's aria "Or sai chi l'onore," Act II with the first finale, Act III with the sextet, which begins with Donna Elvira's words "Sola, sola, in buio loco," and Act IV with the second finale.

21. However, it is not possible to accept the speculation of Abert, who, after rejecting the possibility that Mozart may have had philosophical preoccupations, sees in the drama an antithesis not between guilt and expiation but between Being and Non-being. Similarly forced, although suggestively argued, is the thesis of L. Dallapiccola, "Considerazioni in margine alla scena della statua nel *Don Giovanni,*" in *Appunti incontri meditazioni* (Milan, 1970), that Don Giovanni represents Evil and that his opposite, the Commendatore, is the real protagonist.

22. As was already observed by Dent, *Mozart's Operas*, p. 12. Dent accurately compares the libretti of Bertati and Da Ponte and examines the possibility of other derivations, but he was unacquainted with various other libretti on Don Giovanni. In contrast, Kunze, *Don Giovanni vor Mozart,* who minutely compares Act II of *Il capriccio drammatico* and *Don Giovanni,* practically ignores Molière and Goldoni.

23. Among the latest to do this is Mila, *Lettura del Don Giovanni*, p. 22, who, emphasizing the use of the word *dramma,* adds: "The very fact of having felt the need to modify the traditional phrase *opera comica* . . . shows that the authors realized they had created something out of the ordinary."

24. See Mozart, *Briefe und Aufzeichnungen,* vol. 3, pp. 267-69, letter no. 745, and Anderson, pp. 847-48. It also anticipates the female cast of *Così fan tutte:* Fiordiligi, *seria,* Doralice, *mezzo carattere,* and Despina, *buffa. Le nozze di Figaro* is more complex in this regard, but even there it is possible to view the Countess as the first female *seria* role, Susanna as *mezzo carattere,* and Cherubino (Mozart thought of the voices and not the the the sex of the characters) as *buffa.*

25. On Bassi, see F. D'Amico, "Luigi Bassi," *Enciclopedia dello spettacolo.*

26. Other "mezzi caratteri" who should be noted include the Count in *La villanella rapita* (anticipating the Count in *Le nozze di Figaro*), Henry IV of France in *Il re alla caccia* (libretto by Goldoni) who is comic only because he is seen in the intimate context of everyday life rather than amidst the pomp of his royal station, and Richard the Lionhearted in various Italian adaptations of Grétry's *Richard Cœur de Lion.*

27. See note 19 above.

28. Dent, *Mozart's Operas,* p. 146.

29. This statement belongs to the period of gestation of *Die Entführung,* the first opera in which Mozart realized the fullness of his psychological intuition (with which he evidently prevailed over his librettist); the word "poetry" should be understood in the restricted sense of "libretto," a text in verse that had little to do with true poetry. In spite of every appearance to the contrary, Mozart's position was not very different from Gluck's, who had claimed (using Calzabigi as his mouthpiece) that it was music's office "to serve poetry with expression," but implied in this last phrase that both arts shared a common dramatic and expressive intent.

30. From Mozart's letter to G. von Jacquin of 4 November 1787 we also learn that they wanted him to remain in Prague to write another opera. For Mozart's original see Mozart, *Briefe und Aufzeichnungen,* vol. 4, pp. 58-59, letter no. 1072. For an English translation see Anderson, pp. 912-14.

31. Da Ponte, *Memorie,* p. 131, recounts: "It appeared on stage and . . . must I say it? *Don Giovanni* did not please! . . . Additions were made, some arias were changed, and it was again presented on stage; and *Don Giovanni* did not please. And what did the emperor say of this?—The opera is divine: and perhaps more lovely than *Figaro,* but it is not food for the palates of my Viennese."

Chapter Five: Mozart's *Don Giovanni*

1. Aside from those found in monographs on the life and works of the composer, I note the following: C. Gounod, *Le Don Juan de Mozart* (Paris, 1890), C. Saint-Saëns, *Charles Gounod et le Don Juan de Mozart* (Paris, 1894), R. Dumesnil, *Le Don Juan de Mozart* (Paris, 1927), P. Stefan, *Don Giovanni* (Vienna, 1938), P.-J. Jouve, *Le Don Juan de Mozart* (Freiburg, 1942), P.E. Carapezza, *Figaro e Don Giovanni due folli giornate* (Palermo: Flaccovio, 1974), F. D'Amico, *Intorno al Don Giovanni di Mozart* (Rome: Bulzoni, 1978), which contains in an appendix the analysis of the opera in Abert's *W. A. Mozart* (1919–1920).

2. Mozart wrote upwards of forty symphonies, usually in three or four movements (the three-movement cycles consist of an Allegro, an Andante or Adagio, and an Allegro Finale; those in four movements consist of the same movements with a Minuet inserted before the Finale). The most famous and most often performed Mozart symphonies are the last three, composed during the summer of 1788 and therefore in the period immediately after the composition of *Don Giovanni.* The first movement of a symphony usually has a musical structure that is analogous to the first movement of a sonata or a quartet (and of various other instrumental genres)—a structure referred to as "sonata form," which characterizes the first movement of such compositions (and often also the Finale). A sonata-form movement is basically divided into three sections: the exposition of the two themes (the first in the home key, the other in the dominant, or the relative major in pieces that begin in the minor mode);

the development with elaboration of the two themes and excursions to other keys; and the recapitulation, which restates the exposition modifying it so that the second theme now appears in the home key.

3. A moderate or slow introduction that evolves through unusual harmonic progressions highlighting the release of the rhythm and themes of the Allegro is characteristic of several symphonies, even if Mozart himself rarely adopted this approach. Several authors have hesitated to refer to the beginning of the overture to *Don Giovanni* as an introduction, considering that the term implies an unessential or accessory element. But when a composer of Mozart's stature includes an introduction it is always essential. In this instance, the introduction allows Mozart to establish a connection with the most dramatic aspects of the opera, while the Allegro that follows reflects (without adopting any of the themes) the opera's rhythmic vitality and continuity. The D major that establishes itself soon after the introduction is usually considered the brightest orchestral key, and is an especially brilliant one for the strings.

4. This is a new theme that provides the transition, a function that in other compositions is often fulfilled through musical material that is less sharply characterized thematically. In the development, Mozart highlights the following theme, which better fulfills the function of a secondary theme. It should be kept in mind that the technical formula of sonata form is only an abstraction with respect to the variety of its concrete realizations. It will be seen that the key of A major and the modulations to C major often recur in the pieces most characteristic of Don Giovanni; however, it would be risky to try to establish a correspondence between the themes of the overture and the characters of the opera.

5. Dent, *Mozart's Operas,* p. 157, states that the voices of the trio (with the text in German and only a hint of the accompaniment in thirds) were transcribed by Beethoven in a sketch that lay before him during the composition of the Adagio of the Piano Sonata in c-sharp minor, Op. 27, no. 2 (the so-called Moonlight Sonata).

6. The temporal relationships are unclear, but it would seem logical that the narrated events took place the preceding evening and thus it is

strange that she has not yet completely informed Don Ottavio (but if she had, she would have lost the opportunity of now informing the audience). The narration has come to form the crux of the speculation for and against Donna Anna's—let us say—physical and psychological integrity; but, on a realistic level (if it is at all valid to refer to realism with regard to operatic plots), it can be observed that the assailant would not have been able to achieve his intended goal without losing the cloak that made it impossible for her to recognize him. Don Ottavio's interjections have induced some (for example, Dent, *Mozart's Operas,* pp. 160-161) to hold him up to ridicule.

7. At this point, Mozart repeats textual passages from the second part of the aria in a way that is not very felicitous from the point of view of syntax: "Rammenta la piaga, Rimira *di* sangue" [literally, "Call to mind the wound, Gaze once more *of* the blood"].

8. The dramatically unnecessary broadening of the closing section is explained if, as Dent has suggested, this aria was intended as the close of Act I.

9. Both Lorenzi and Bertati had already played in various ways with the diminutive "Don Giovannino," which at this point expresses excessive familiarity.

10. Curiously, Jouve, *Le Don Juan de Mozart,* p. 100, describes the beginning of this scene as follows: "Don Juan receives the news of the intrigue while preparing his toilette; he paints his face and puts luxurious white gloves on his hands." All of this would take place in the open (the stage set is still the "quarter next to Don Giovanni's palace" where the peasants danced), and there is no indication of this in the libretto. It must stem from some imagined staging, and the same is true of the champagne glass in the hand of the protagonist, from which this aria derives its name.

11. Today's theatrical conventions according to which characters played by baritones are never the youngest and most robust would lead us to misunderstand Don Giovanni.

12. This is not, however, as some have claimed, the "unfolding of one chord," nor is it harmonically empty, supported only by the rhythm. Naturally, the faster the pace, the more schematic the harmonies become.

13. This is true, because the formal act of "giving her hand" would have taken place indoors, but it is not the whole truth. This is one of the traits Zerlina shares with Goldoni's Elisa.

14. The original score does not indicate Allegro, but it is natural for the passage in 6/8 to be faster. Formally, this second part can only be considered a closing section, since it does not depart from the key of F major. A particularly refined touch is the use of a solo cello obbligato as a continuous accompaniment to the vocal part, a touch that Gazzaniga also employed in the last aria of his Donna Elvira.

15. The unique superimposition of three orchestras in different dance rhythms seems to me to be a suggestion Da Ponte drew from Beaumarchais's *Tarare,* where at a certain point he calls for a "marche dont le dessus léger peint le caractère des Bergers de Cour qui la dansent, et dont la basse peint la lourde gaïeté des Paysans qui la sautent" ["a march in which the treble depicts the character of the shepherds who dance to it, and in which the bass depicts the heavy gaiety of the peasants who jump about to its rhythm"]; see my essay "Causerie su Beaumarchais e la musica teatrale" in *Scelte poetiche di musicisti* (Venice: Marsilio, 1987), pp. 309-21. In performance (and even more so in recordings) the second and third orchestras rarely manage to be heard over the persistent minuet of the first orchestra.

16. The indication in the score is "night," which is more logical than the indication in the libretto at the beginning of scene ii, "night gradually comes on." The latter makes it seem as if an entire day has passed without Don Giovanni speaking with Leporello about the events that occurred in Act I.

17. Bertati may already have borrowed the idea for scene x from Lorenzi's libretto for Tritto.

18. It is usually claimed that the cut derives from the vocal deficiencies of the new tenor, but none of scene x makes any sense (and had to be cut) because of the Viennese addition of three scenes that will be discussed in the note that follows.

19. These scenes include Zerlina's attempt to prevent Leporello from escaping by threatening him and tying him to a chair, from which he later succeeds in freeing himself—the first scene is in recitative, part of which is accompanied by the orchestra, the second is an extended duet, and the third is a recitative for Leporello. All of this indicates how the Viennese version emphasizes the comic aspect of the opera.

20. Caterina Cavalieri, a Viennese singer who was a pupil of Mozart's, had played the role of Costanze in *Die Entführung* in 1782; while he was preparing that work, Mozart already confessed having made concessions because of the singer's flexible throat (in a letter to his father dated 26 September 1781). Cavalieri and Mozart's sister-in-law, Aloysia Lange, who sang the roles of Donna Elvira and Donna Anna in Vienna, had already sung for Mozart in the one-act singspiel *Der Schauspieldirektor* in February 1786.

21. This should be a continuation of the night that began with the serenade below Donna Elvira's balcony. Don Giovanni tells the time from the clock ("it is not yet two o'clock at night") and immediately afterward asks how "the affair between Leporello and Donna Elvira went." It is useless to point to the usual incongruity of a tomb that has already been built and provided with an inscription.

22. Only at this point do Don Giovanni and Leporello take back their own clothes. Modern libretti do not usually retain the above-mentioned variant in the Viennese libretto.

23. Dent, *Mozart's Operas,* p. 169, believes the trombones were not placed in the orchestra but rather backstage. The statue's admonishment, "You shall stop laughing before the dawn," leads one to believe that all the events that follow occur in the same night.

24. I find unacceptable the claim of Dallapiccola, "Considerazioni," pp. 45-46, that the graveyard scene (which never becomes a trio) is the symmetrical counterweight to the truly tragic trio of Act I, scene i. (His essay is, nevertheless, rich in astute observations.)

25. According to Dent, *Mozart's Operas,* p. 171, the only point to this scene is to provide an aria for Donna Anna. It disturbs Dallapiccola, "Considerazioni," pp. 47-48, because it destroys the symmetry he believes exists between the beginning and end of the opera (he cites the negative judgments of Berlioz and Kierkegaard, which were also connected to preconceived motivations); but if the negative judgements are legitimate and understandable, it is more perplexing to understand Toscanini's curt declaration (referred to by Dallapiccola) that he always omitted Donna Anna's aria (or the entire scene?). Even recognizing what Mila calls the craftsmanlike attitude of Mozart (but what craftsmanship!) and the practice of his time of introducing changes to an opera for each production, to what point can we today, even with the best intentions, touch up a work of the past?

26. There may have been additional reasons: for example, that of introducing an element of contrast between the comic duet of scene xii and the new buffoonery of scene xv. It should also be noted that each of the female parts has an aria of this type: Zerlina in Act I, scene xiii (also in F major), and Donna Elvira in scene xi.

27. Although the theme has all the characteristics of a rondo theme, it is presented only twice, framing a single contrasting episode.

28. As I have already mentioned, the final scene was omitted in the Viennese performances of 1788.

29. It is interesting to see here reproduced on the stage a characteristic of the musical practices of the day, the use of music on the part of the high aristocracy during every aspect of their daily life, during receptions, banquets and garden parties. Here Don Giovanni's small orchestra performs pieces from well-known operas, but much symphonic music and chamber music was expressly composed to be used in this way.

30. The opera by Martin y Soler, to a libretto by Bertati, was performed in
    Vienna in 1786 and rapidly eclipsed *Le nozze di Figaro*. Sarti's opera, to a
    libretto by Goldoni, enjoyed great success in Vienna in 1783 under the
    title *I due litiganti*.

31. Dallapiccola, "Considerazioni," does not underscore the point that
    Donna Elvira's scream coincides with the diminished seventh chord to
    which he attaches particular importance (see the note that follows). As
    we will learn in the final scene, she screams because she has seen a ghost
    in the dark, and the same chord, transposed a whole step higher, is
    repeated for Leporello's cry (upon seeing much more than Elvira, of
    which he gives a confused account in the Allegro molto).

32. Dallapiccola, "Considerazioni," bases his recognition of symmetrical par-
    allels between the moment the Commendatore is murdered and the
    moment his image (the symbol of Good) is presented to the murderer
    (the personification of Evil) on the fact that the first chord of scene xvii
    is a repetition of the same chord that precedes the trio that closes Act I,
    scene i (the murder of the Commendatore). But this chord, a diminished
    seventh, is among the most common in the harmonic language of the
    time, and furthermore it is the same in the two instances singled out by
    Dallapiccola only in the sonority and not in the spelling, since Mozart
    uses it in two different harmonic contexts—in the first instance leading
    to the c minor of the trio, in the second instance leading toward a resolu-
    tion in d minor.

33. It should be kept in mind that Mozart first conceived these themes for
    the scene in the body of the opera, and only later, when he came to write
    out the overture, did he use them as the introduction there.

34. It is impossible to ignore Darius Milhaud's observation (referred to by
    Dallapiccola, "Considerazioni," p. 59) that this phrase encompasses all
    twelve pitches of the chromatic scale in the course of five measures, a
    practice that only in our own century was established as a compositional
    method, labelled dodecaphonic. One may still doubt what conclusions
    should be drawn from this observation.

35. With characteristically rich suggestiveness, Dallapiccola, "Considerazioni," pp. 43-44 and 57, points to these drawn-out intervals of the Commendatore's vocal part as "an anticipation of what in our century would be called expressionistic writing."

36. There is a parallel between the Commendatore's phrase here and the way it is presented at the beginning of the overture; but the melodic line in the overture, which descends by octave leaps and ascends by fifths or fourths, is distorted here (the descending intervals are a seventh and a diminished fifth, the ascending intervals are half steps).

37. It seems to me useless to psychoanalyze an operatic character through the libretto. The entire tradition from *El burlador* onward makes no reference to Donna Anna's mother; this clearly accentuates her connection to her surviving parent.

38. In Ernst Theodor Hoffman's brief account of an imaginary encounter with Donna Anna, she herself mentions this aria: "when, instead of feeling and understanding my soul, the public applauds me because of a difficult scale passage or graceful *fioritura,* it seems to me that an iron hand is about to crush my heart" (*Phantasiestücke in Callots Manier* [Fantasy Pieces in the Style of Callot]).

39. Apart from the fact that Mozart and Da Ponte were commissioned to write another comic opera for Prague, it must be kept in mind that for the public of the time *Don Giovanni* was not, as it is today, a costume drama; it would have been difficult if not impossible to make it conform to the conventions of *opera seria.* Even sixty years later in *La traviata,* Verdi was particularly daring in choosing a subject deriving from a celebrated novel in a contemporary setting.

40. For Da Ponte the most obvious and spontaneous derivation must have been from "lepus" (lepidità [witticism]); it is unlikely that, as has been suggested, he thought of Lipperl, a substitute for Kasperl, or Käsperle, as the German equivalent of Arlecchino.

41. A term used by Mila, *Lettura del Don Giovanni,* p. 59.

42. All the psychological and metapsychological interpretations of Jouve, *Le Don Juan de Mozart,* pp. 148-149, are unnecessary to make this a shameful act.

43. Macchia, *Vita avventure,* pp. 56-60, dedicates several pages, entitled "Il 'cupio dissolvi,'" to one such interpretation, that of Nikolaus Lenau.

EXAMPLES

Esempio 1. L'Empio punito. Atto I, 3, recitativo di Atamira

Esempio 2. L'Empio punito. Atto I, 5, aria di Atamira

ge - te.   Ma se un A - stro ri - go - ro - so

Non dà tre - gua,   non dà tre - gua al suo fu - ro - re

Sot - to l' a - le del ri - po - so   Tro - vi pa - ce il

mio   do - lo _____ - re.   Sot - to

207

Esempio 3. L'Empio punito. Atto 1, 9, duetto

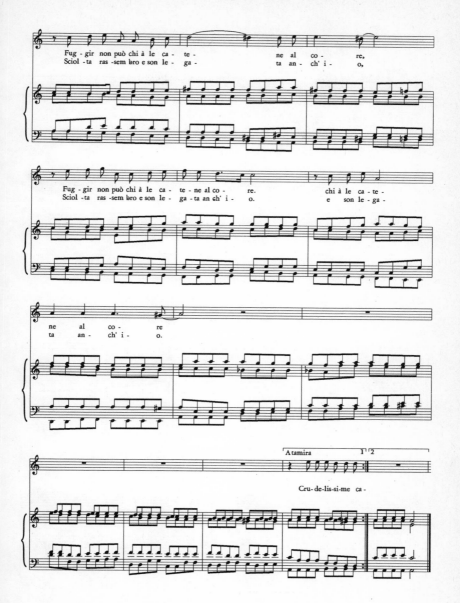

Esempio 4. L'Empio punito. Atto II, 14, aria e recitativo

sen l' a - ni - ma mi_____ - a.

Violini

Su, di - le - gua - te - vi, Lar - ve d' A -

Continuo

mor, Su, se - pa -

Violini

Continuo

ra - te - vi, Spir - ti del cor, Per - ché a du - el - lo e -

Esempio 5. L'Empio punito. Atto II, 1, arietta di Delfa

Al de - sio la li - ber - tà, la li - ber - tà.

Violini

Esempio 6. L'Empio punito. Atto II, 19, arietta di Cloridoro

Esempio 7. L'Empio punito. Atto II, *22, duetto*

220

Esempio 8. Il Convitato di pietra. Sc. 1, serenata e scena

Mo' ven - go a ba - scio ca la si - gno - ra, che la si - gno - ra che cuol - lo ha

n' uoc - chio.

fat - to pe v' a - spet - tà, che cuol - lo ha fat - to pe v' a - spet - tà

Don Giovanni

Vi - ci - no è il So - le, Spun - ta l' au - ro - ra,

230

Esempio 9. Il Convitato di pietra. Sc. 4, recitativo e aria

235

D. Anna

Per - fi - da! io dun - que so - no La

bar - ba - ra ca - gion del - la sua mor - te! Ah, qua - le il mio de -

lit - to, e - ter - ni de - i, A _ pre or - ri - bi - le sce - na a - gli oc - chi - mie - i!

ARIA: D. Anna

O - ve lo

[Andantino]

cor, non tras - se an - cor, Fa - te - lovo - i al - me - no, Ri -

mor - si del mio cor. Fa - te - lo voi, voi al -

me - no, Ri - mor - si del mio cor, del mio cor,

del mio cor, Ri - mor - si del mio

Esempio 10. Il Convitato di pietra. Sc. 10, concertato

Esempio 11. Il Convitato di pietra. Sc. 13, aria di Lesbina

INDEX

index